LEARN TO
Bead Jewellery

Antique Cross Set, page 26

www.companyscoming.com
visit our website

Front Cover: Asian Style, page 38

Learn to Bead Jewellery

Copyright © Company's Coming Publishing Limited

First Printing November 2009

Library and Archives Canada Cataloguing in Publication
Learn to bead jewellery.
(Company's Coming crafts)
Includes index.
ISBN 978-1-897477-23-6
1. Beadwork. 2. Jewelry making. I. Title: Bead jewellery. II. Series: Company's coming crafts
TT860.L43 2009   745.58'2   C2009-901983-3

Published by
Company's Coming Publishing Limited
2311-96 Street
Edmonton, Alberta, Canada T6N 1G3
Tel: 780-450-6223   Fax: 780-450-1857
www.companyscoming.com

Printed in China

The Company's Coming Story

Jean Paré grew up with an understanding that family, friends and home cooking are the key ingredients for a good life. A mother of four, Jean worked as a professional caterer for 18 years, operating out of her home kitchen. During that time, she came to appreciate quick and easy recipes that call for everyday ingredients. In answer to mounting requests for her recipes, Company's Coming cookbooks were born, and Jean moved on to a new chapter in her career.

Company's Coming founder Jean Paré

Just as Company's Coming continues to promote the tradition of home cooking, the same is now true with crafting. Like good cooking, great craft results depend upon easy-to-follow instructions, readily available materials and enticing photographs of the finished products. Also like cooking, crafting is meant to be enjoyed in the home or cottage. Company's Coming Crafts, then, is a natural extension from the kitchen into the family room or den.

In the beginning, Jean worked from a spare bedroom in her home, located in the small prairie town of Vermilion, Alberta, Canada. The first Company's Coming cookbook, *150 Delicious Squares*, was an immediate bestseller. Today, with well over 150 titles in print, Company's Coming has earned the distinction of publishing Canada's most popular cookbooks. The company continues to gain new supporters by adhering to Jean's "Golden Rule of Cooking"—Never share a recipe you wouldn't use yourself. It's an approach that has worked—millions of times over!

Company's Coming cookbooks are distributed throughout Canada, the United States, Australia and other international English-language markets. French and Spanish language editions have also been published. Sales to date have surpassed 25 million copies with no end in sight. Familiar and trusted in home kitchens around the world, Company's Coming cookbooks are highly regarded both as kitchen workbooks and as family heirlooms.

Because Company's Coming operates a test kitchen and not a craft shop, we've partnered with a major North American craft content publisher to assemble a variety of craft compilations exclusively for us. Our editors have been involved every step of the way. You can see the excellent results for yourself in the book you're holding.

Company's Coming Crafts are for everyone—whether you're a beginner or a seasoned pro. What better gift could you offer than something you've made yourself? In these hectic days, people still enjoy crafting parties; they bring family and friends together in the same way a good meal does. Company's Coming is proud to support crafters with this new creative book series.

We hope you enjoy these easy-to-follow, informative and colourful books, and that they inspire your creativity. So, don't delay—get crafty!

TABLE OF CONTENTS

Cleopatra's Collar, 60

Asian Style, 38

Frosted Ice & Silver, 66

TABLE OF CONTENTS

Butterfly Garden, 110

Carved Carnelian, 75

Wisdom & Mirth, 72

Mermaid Magic, 104

Feeling Crafty? Get Creative!

Each 160-page book features easy-to-follow, step-by-step instructions and full-page colour photographs of every project. Whatever your crafting fancy, there's a Company's Coming Creative Series craft book to match!

Beading: Beautiful Accessories in Under an Hour

Complement your wardrobe, give your home extra flair or add an extra-special personal touch to gifts with these quick and easy beading projects. Create any one of these special crafts in an hour or less.

Knitting: Easy Fun for Everyone

Take a couple of needles and some yarn and see what beautiful things you can make! Learn how to make fashionable sweaters, comfy knitted blankets, scarves, bags and other knitted crafts with these easy to intermediate knitting patterns.

Card Making: Handmade Greetings for All Occasions

Making your own cards is a fun, creative and inexpensive way of letting someone know you care. Stamp, emboss, quill or layer designs in a creative and unique card with your own personal message for friends or family.

Patchwork Quilting

In this book full of throws, baby quilts, table toppers, wall hangings—and more—you'll find plenty of beautiful projects to try. With the modern fabrics available, and the many practical and decorative applications, patchwork quilting is not just for Grandma!

Crocheting: Easy Blankets, Throws & Wraps

Find projects perfect for decorating your home, for looking great while staying warm or for giving that one-of-a-kind gift. A range of simple but stunning designs make crocheting quick, easy and entertaining.

Sewing: Fun Weekend Projects

Find a wide assortment of easy and attractive projects to help you create practical storage solutions, decorations for any room or just the right gift for that someone special. Create table runners, placemats, baby quilts, pillows and more!

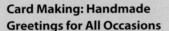

FOREWORD

As you flip through this 128-page book you'll be sure to catch the "beading bug" that is sweeping the country. It seems that jewellery accessories are in every store. By stringing your own jewellery, you'll create just the right touch to complement your wardrobe. Because beading is so popular, there are beading shops everywhere. Large craft stores are adorning their aisles with beautiful, luscious beading components that are sure to call your name. If you're like many people, you might already have quite the stash of jewellery components and are just waiting to string them into dazzling designs you'll be proud to wear.

We've included splendid designs just for you in three different skill levels from beginner to intermediate. The book is divided into four chapters—Casual Complements, Out on the Town, Trendy Temptations and Alluring Fun. You'll find many stunning necklaces, dazzling bracelets, deliciously fun earrings, sophisticated watches and more. There are projects suitable for wearing with barely-there summer attire and with chunky winter sweaters, with elegant party attire and with casual jeans.

With our helpful visual glossary, easy step-by-step instructions, full-colour photography and your own creativity, it won't take long until you are making beautiful bead creations for your wardrobe. Find a design you love and decide whether you want to follow the design as is or change one of the elements—size, colour, texture, materials or theme. It can be intimidating to alter a design, but once you've been beading for a while, you'll soon be making jewellery to match every outfit you wear.

Bounty of Buttons, page 112

Each design included in this book has a complementary piece so you will not only have a necklace, but also a pair of earrings or bracelet to match. Many of our irresistible designs can be made—start to finish—in a half hour or so. A few will take a little more time, but you'll think they're well worth it when you start receiving compliments about your jewellery. It will make you proud to be able to say thanks for the kind words and tell your friends you made it yourself.

So, what are you waiting for? With our photo index in the back of this book, you'll be able to see at a glance all the beautiful and dazzling designs we've included just for you. Get out your bead stash or drive to the nearest bead store, where you can select stunning beading components to make one of our beautiful designs. We've also included a source listing with each set of instructions.

No matter what the occasion is, you'll be dressed in style with beautiful jewellery you've made yourself.

VISUAL GLOSSARY

Tools

Crimping pliers are used for just what their name implies —crimping! The back slot puts a seam in the middle of the crimp tube, separating the ends of the flex wire and trapping it firmly. The front slot rounds out the tube and turns it into a small, tidy bead.

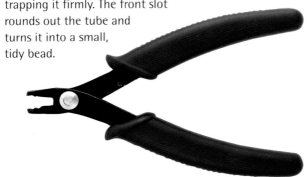

Round-nose pliers are intended for turning round loops. They do not work well for holding or grasping since they tend to leave a small dent.

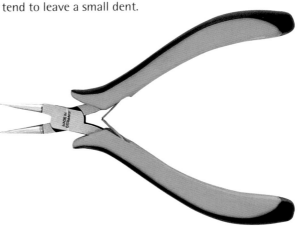

Chain-nose pliers are the most useful tool in your entire toolbox. For holding, opening and closing jump rings and bending sharp angles.

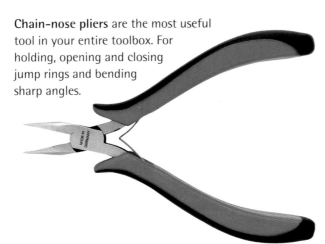

Flat-nose pliers are a wire power tool. They are excellent for turning sharp corners, holding items and for opening and closing jump rings.

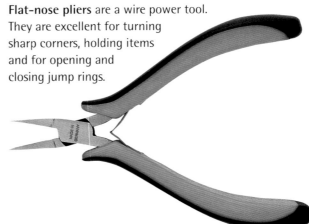

Wire flush cutters leave one flat side and one pointed side on each cut. Using flush cutters is especially important when working with heavy gauges of wire (20-gauge or smaller). One side of the cutter is flat, and the other is indented.

A bench block is a flat, smooth piece of hardened steel. Hammering on top of a block flattens out and hardens the wire. Bench blocks are also used for stamping metal to get a clean impression.

Materials

Eye Pins are wires with a loop on one end and a straight portion of wire where beads can be strung. Length and gauges vary; most earrings use 24-gauge eye pins from 1½–2½ inches.

Nylon-jaw pliers can be used to harden or straighten wire.

A head pin is a piece of wire with a stop end like a fine nail head. A bead slides onto the head pin and stops on the head. Lengths and gauges vary; most earrings use 24-gauge head pins from 1½–2½ inches.

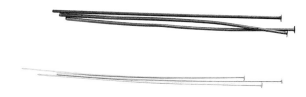

Jeweller's hammers have fine, smooth curved heads to leave a clean impression. The round peen side works well for texturing wire and metal sheet.

Jump rings are one of the most versatile findings used in jewellery making. They come in all sizes, gauges and metals. They are measured by diameter (width) and gauge (weight).

Ear wires come in many different styles. Regular fishhook style are the most common and the easiest to make yourself. Recommended weight for ear wires is either 22- or 20-gauge.

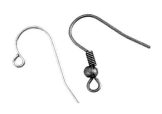

Crimp tubes are small, soft metal cylinders that can be flattened or formed around flexible beading wire to secure the ends. They are an essential component for bead-stringing projects.

Wire comes in many sizes or *gauges*. Gauge is the measured diameter of the wire. The higher the number, the thinner the wire. Wire can be tempered soft, half-hard or hard, which refers to its stiffness. Copper, silver and gold-filled are most commonly used for jewellery.

Flexible beading wire comes in several weights from .010–.026-inch-diameter and is designed for stringing. It is available in precious metal and several colours and is made from 7 to 49 strands of steel wire, twisted and encased in a flexible plastic coating. Ends are finished with crimp beads using either crimping or chain-nose pliers.

BASICS STEP BY STEP

Opening & Closing Jump Rings

Jump rings are one of the most versatile findings used in jewellery making. They come in all sizes and gauges.

Use two pairs of smooth chain-nose pliers (bent or flat-nose pliers work fine as second pliers) (Photo A).

Photo A

Push ring open with right pliers while holding across the ring with left pliers. To close, hold in the same way and rock the ring back and forth until ring ends rub against

Photo B

each other or you hear a click. Moving the ring past closed then back hardens the ring and assures a tight closure (Photo B).

Making an Eye Pin or Round Loop

Eye pins should be made with half-hard wire to make sure they hold their shape; 22-gauge will fit through most beads, with the exception of many semiprecious stones. Most Czech glass beads and 4mm crystals will fit on 20-gauge wire.

The length used for the eye loop depends on how big you want the loop. Here we will use ⅜ inch for a moderate-size loop.

Flush-trim end of wire (Photo C).

Photo C

Photo D

Using chain-nose pliers, make a 90-degree bend ⅜ inch from end of wire (Photo D).

Using round-nose pliers, grasp the end of the wire so no wire sticks out between plier blades (Photo E).

Photo E

Begin making a loop by rolling your hand away from your body. Don't try to make the entire loop in one movement. Roll your hand a one-quarter turn counterclockwise (Photo F).

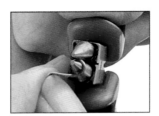

Photo F

Without removing pliers from loop, open plier blade slightly and pivot pliers back toward your body clockwise about a one-quarter turn (Photo G).

Photo G

Close pliers onto the wire and roll the loop until it comes around, next to the 90-degree bend (Photo H).

Photo H

Open and close eye-pin loops the same way as jump rings, by pushing open front to back (Photo I).

Photo I

Making Wire-Wrapped Loops

Practice wrapping wire with either 22- or 24-gauge wire. Harden slightly by pulling on one end with the other end clamped in a vise or pull one or two times through nylon-jaw pliers (Photo J).

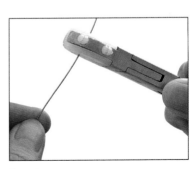

Photo J

Make a 90-degree bend about 1½ inches from end of the wire using chain-nose pliers (Photo K).

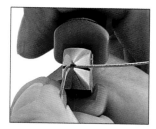

Photo K

Using round-nose pliers, grab wire about ⅜ inch away from the 90-degree and roll your hand away from yourself, toward the bend until a loop is halfway formed (Photos L and M).

Photo L

Photo M

Without removing pliers from forming loop, open the jaw and rotate pliers clockwise about a one-quarter turn (Photo N).

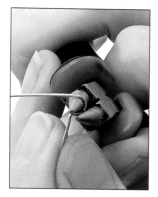

Photo N

Grab the end of the wire with your left (or non-dominant) hand and pull it around the rest of the way until it crosses itself and completes the loop (Photo O).

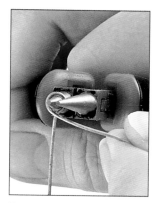

Photo O

Switch to chain-nose pliers, holding across the loop. Wrap tail around wire under loop with your left hand. If you are using a heavy gauge of wire, it is often easier to use a second pliers to pull the tail around instead of your fingers (Photos P and Q).

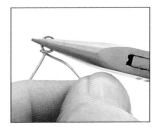

Photo P

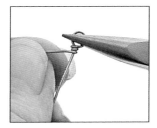

Photo Q

Flush-cut wire as close to the wrap as possible. Tuck end down if needed, using chain-nose pliers (Photos R and S).

Photo R

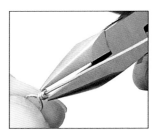

Photo S

To create a wrap on the opposite end of the bead, leave a gap equal to wrap space on first end. Grasp to the right of the wrap space and make a 90-degree bend (Photos T and U).

Photo T

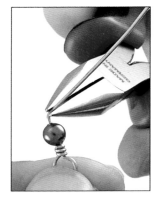

Photo U

Repeat from Photo L to Photo U to complete.

Hammering Wire

Hammering hardens and flattens round wire. This can be especially important when making ear wires or clasps that need to hold their shape. Always use a smooth, hardened steel surface to guarantee a clean finish. Any marks or scars on a bench block or hammer will impress on the surface of wire or sheet metal.

Create your shape from wire. Keep hammer flat to prevent marring wire. Flip over after a few taps and hammer on opposite side. Don't get carried away; if you hammer too much, metal becomes brittle and breaks (Photo V).

Photo V

Crimping

String a crimp bead onto flexible wire. String clasp or ring and pass tail of flexible wire back through crimp to form a loop.

Hold wires parallel and make sure crimp is positioned correctly. Using front slot on pliers, shape crimp into a small oval (Photo W).

Photo W

Put oval into back slot of pliers and squeeze to make fold in the centre with one wire on each side of fold (Photo X).

Photo X

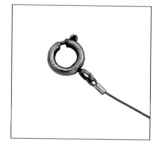

Photo Y

Return to front slot, and squeeze again to tighten crimp. Do a few more rotations and squeezes to solidify and shape crimp bead. Trim wire tail (Photo Y).

A THOUSAND FLOWERS

This lovely bracelet and earring set will wrap you in a thousand flowers of delight each time you wear them.

Design | Caito Amorose

Skill Level
Intermediate

Finished Sizes
Earrings: 2½ inches long
Bracelet: 7 inches (including clasp)

Materials
18 (6mm) mother-of-pearl round beads
9 (15mm) millefiori hearts
4mm Austrian crystal bicone beads: 8 red, 10 cobalt blue
14 (.021-inch-diameter) sterling silver head pins
6 (.021-inch-diameter) sterling silver eye pins
9 (4mm) sterling silver jump rings
2 sterling silver French ear wires
Sterling silver spring-ring clasp with
    6mm closed ring
32 inches 24-gauge
    sterling silver wire
Round-nose pliers
Chain-nose pliers
Wire nippers

Earrings

1) Slide a mother-of-pearl bead onto an eye pin; form a wrapped loop above bead. Trim excess wire. Open loop on ear wire and slide on eye pin; close loop.

2) Slide a red crystal onto an eye pin; form a wrapped loop above crystal, attaching loop to bottom loop below mother-of-pearl bead before wrapping. Trim excess wire.

3) Slide a cobalt blue crystal onto an eye pin and form a wrapped loop above crystal, attaching loop to previous loop before wrapping. Trim excess wire.

4) Open bottom loop and slide on a heart; close loop.

5) Slide a red crystal onto a head pin; form a wrapped loop above crystal. Trim excess wire. Repeat twice, once with another red crystal and once with a cobalt blue crystal. Open a jump ring and slide on assembled head pins; attach jump ring to bottom link below mother-of-pearl bead. Close jump ring.

6) Repeat steps 1–5 for second earring.

Thousand Flowers
Millefiori hearts, beads and findings
from Fire Mountain Gems and Beads.

Bracelet

1) Cut 16 (2-inch) lengths of 24-gauge sterling silver wire.

2) Use round-nose pliers to form a wrapped loop ½ inch from one end on one length of wire, attaching loop to one half of clasp before wrapping. Slide on a mother-of-pearl bead. Form another wrapped loop. Trim excess wire.

3) Repeat step 2, only attach loop to previous loop before wrapping. Continue in the same manner until all 16 wire lengths have been connected, attaching last loop to remaining half of clasp before wrapping.

4) Open a jump ring and slide on a heart; repeat six additional times. Attach hearts, evenly spaced, to bracelet.

5) Slide a red crystal onto a head pin; begin to form a loop above bead, but do not wrap loop yet. Repeat seven additional times, three times with red crystals and four times with cobalt blue crystals.

6) Attach head pins from step 5 onto bracelet by wrapping loops onto bracelet, spacing them as desired. Trim excess wire. ■

FRESH SQUEEZED

Sunshine colours play counterpoint to the cool allure of the sea in this gorgeous set created in carnelian and honey jade.

Design | Dianne de Vienne

Skill Level
Easy

Finished Sizes
Necklace: 15¾ inches (including clasp)
Earrings: 2 inches long

Materials
44mm carnelian disc bead
10 carnelian nuggets
4 (8mm) carnelian round beads
24 (8mm) serpentine rondelle beads
12 (8mm) honey jade round beads
18 (4–5mm) gold vermeil daisy spacers
2 gold-filled crimp beads
Gold-filled head pins: 1 (3-inch),
    2 (2½-inch)
2 gold-filled ear wires
Gold vermeil toggle clasp
22 inches .018-inch-diameter
    nylon-coated flexible beading wire
Round-nose pliers
Chain-nose pliers
Wire nippers

Necklace

1) Set aside two carnelian nuggets to be used for earrings.

2) Slide the following onto the 3-inch head pin: daisy spacer, carnelian disc and a daisy spacer. Use round-nose pliers to form a wrapped loop above top spacer. Trim excess wire. Set aside to be used later.

3) String a crimp bead ½ inch from one end of wire. Place wire end through one half of clasp and back through crimp bead. Use crimp pliers to flatten and fold crimp bead.

4) String three daisy spacers and two carnelian round beads onto wire.

Fresh Squeezed

Carnelian nuggets from Alko Rock Shop;
daisy spacers from Fire Mountain Gems and
Beads; head pins, ear wires and beading wire
from South Pacific Wholesale Co.

5) String a serpentine rondelle, honey jade round, serpentine rondelle and a carnelian nugget; repeat three additional times. String a serpentine rondelle, honey jade round and a serpentine rondelle.

6) String two daisy spacers, beaded head pin from step 2 and two daisy spacers.

7) Repeat steps 4 and 5, only in reverse, to complete remaining half of necklace.

8) String a crimp bead; place wire end through remaining half of clasp and back through crimp bead and several other beads. Flatten and fold crimp bead. Trim excess wire.

Earrings

1) String the following onto a 2½-inch head pin: daisy spacer, carnelian nugget, daisy spacer, serpentine rondelle, honey jade round, serpentine rondelle and a daisy spacer. Use round-nose pliers to form a loop above top bead; trim excess wire.

2) Open loop on head pin and slide it onto ear wire; close loop.

3) Repeat steps 1 and 2 for second earring. ■

CLASSY COIN PEARLS

A few coin pearls and some black rubber tubing combine to make this simple set that's perfect for summer.

Design | Molly Schaller

Skill Level
Easy

Finished Sizes
Necklace: 14 inches (including clasp)
Bracelet: 6¾ inches (including clasp)

Materials
6 (10mm) white coin pearls
12 (2mm) sterling silver round beads
20 (1.2 x 3.5mm) sterling silver Bali-style spacer beads
4 silver crimp beads
2 (6mm) sterling silver soldered jump rings
2 (13mm) silver-plated lobster-claw clasps
15–20 inches 1.7mm black rubber tubing
24–28 inches .018-inch-diameter nylon-coated flexible beading wire
Crimp pliers
Wire nippers

Necklace

1) Cut a 16-inch length of beading wire. Cut two 5-inch lengths of rubber tubing.

2) String a crimp bead onto wire ½ inch from one end; place short wire end through a lobster-claw clasp and back through crimp bead. Use crimp pliers to flatten and fold crimp bead.

3) String a silver round bead, silver spacer, 5-inch length of rubber tubing and a silver spacer.

4) String a silver round bead, silver spacer, coin pearl and a silver spacer; repeat four additional times. String a silver round bead.

5) Repeat step 3 in reverse.

6) String a crimp bead; place wire end through a jump ring and back through crimp bead, silver round bead and silver spacer. Pull to tighten wire loop. Flatten and fold crimp bead. Trim excess wire.

Bracelet

1) Cut an 8-inch length of beading wire. Cut two 2½-inch lengths of rubber tubing.

2) String a crimp bead onto wire ½ inch from one end; place short wire end through lobster-claw clasp and back through crimp bead. Flatten and fold crimp bead.

3) String a silver round bead, silver spacer, 2½-inch length of rubber tubing, silver spacer and a silver round bead.

4) String a silver spacer, coin pearl and a silver spacer.

5) Repeat step 3.

Classy Coin Pearls
Coin pearls, round beads, spacers, crimp beads, jump rings and clasps from Fire Mountain Gems and Beads; rubber tubing and beading wire from Beadalon.

6) String a crimp bead; place wire end through a jump ring and back through crimp bead, silver round bead and silver spacer. Pull to tighten wire loop. Flatten and fold crimp bead. Trim excess wire. ■

PINKIE SWEAR

Make this lovely duo for yourself and a best friend; then you can pinkie-swear to be friends forever.

Design | Sandy Parpart

Skill Level
Beginner

Finished Sizes
Bracelet: 8 inches (including clasp)
Earrings: 1¾ inches long

Materials
7 (6mm) light rose crystal cube beads
Crystal bicone beads: 14 (6mm) light rose,
   8 (4mm) clear
Sterling silver round beads: 2 (3mm), 2 (2mm)
14 (4mm) sterling silver daisy spacers
14 (5 x 3mm) sterling silver bead caps
2 (3.4mm) sterling silver jump rings
2 (1½-inch) 24-gauge silver head pins
2 (1.3mm) silver crimp beads
2 silver lever-back ear wires
15 x 17mm silver heart toggle clasp
10 inches .018-inch-diameter 7-strand
   nylon-coated flexible beading wire
Round-nose pliers
Flat-nose pliers
Crimp pliers
Wire nippers

Bracelet

1) String a crimp bead onto beading wire ½ inch from one end; place short wire end through one half of clasp and back through crimp bead. Use crimp pliers to flatten and fold crimp bead.

2) String a 3mm sterling silver round bead. String the following: 6mm light rose bicone bead, daisy spacer, 4mm clear bicone bead, daisy spacer, 6mm light rose bicone bead, bead cap, light rose cube bead and a bead cap; repeat four additional times. String a 6mm light rose bicone bead, daisy spacer, 4mm clear bicone bead, daisy spacer, 6mm light rose bicone bead and a 3mm sterling silver round bead.

3) String a crimp bead and remaining half of clasp; place wire end back through crimp bead and several other beads. Flatten and fold crimp bead. Trim excess wire.

Earrings

1) Slide the following onto a head pin: 2mm sterling silver round bead, bead cap, light rose cube bead, bead cap, 6mm light rose bicone bead, daisy spacer and a 4mm clear bicone bead. Use round-nose pliers to form a loop above top bead; trim excess wire. Repeat once.

2) Use jump rings to attach beaded head pins to ear wires. ■

Pinkie Swear
Crimp beads and beading
wire from Beadalon.

ANTIQUE CROSS SET

A Celtic cross pendant becomes a family heirloom when strung with genuine iolite and onyx beads.

Design | Katie Hacker

Skill Level
Beginner

Finished Sizes
Necklace: 16 inches (including clasp)
Earrings: 1¼ inches long

Materials
38 (10mm) iolite oval beads
4 (6mm) onyx round beads
8 (5mm) silver spacers
2 (8mm) silver beads
2 (1.5mm) silver crimp beads
1¼-inch silver Celtic cross pendant
2 silver head pins
2 silver ear wires
Silver lobster-claw clasp and tag
17 inches .018-inch-diameter 19-strand
  nylon-coated flexible beading wire
Round-nose pliers
Crimp pliers
Wire nippers

Necklace

1) String a crimp bead ½ inch from one end of beading wire; thread short wire end through clasp and back through crimp bead. Use crimp pliers to fold crimp bead in half.

2) String 16 iolite beads.

3) String the following: silver spacer, onyx bead, silver spacer and iolite bead; repeat pattern.

4) String a cross pendant. Repeat step 3 in reverse.

5) String 16 iolite beads.

6) String a crimp bead. Thread wire through clasp's tag and back through crimp bead. Crimp the crimp bead. Trim excess wire.

Earrings

1) Place an iolite bead and a silver bead onto a head pin; use round-nose pliers to form a wrapped loop above silver bead, attaching loop to ear wire before wrapping.

2) Repeat step 1 for second earring. ■

Antique Cross

Pendant from Shipwreck Beads; iolite and onyx beads from Thunderbird Supply Co.; crimp beads, clasp and beading wire from Beadalon.

PRETTY IN PINK

Etched shell pendants receive star treatment in this simple necklace and earring set.

Design | Katie Hacker

Skill Level
Beginner

Finished Sizes
Necklace: 20 inches (including clasp)
Earrings: 3¼ inches long

Materials
Pink/white shell pendants: 1 (1¾-inch), 2 (1-inch)
6 (6mm) white cat's-eye round beads
2 (8mm) rose quartz round beads
6 (8mm) rose CRYSTALLIZED™ - Swarovski Elements
   bicone crystals
4 (6mm) silver jump rings
4 silver c-crimp cord ends
2 silver crimp ends
2 silver ear wires
Silver duet clasp
14 inches pink faux-suede lace
2 (1-inch) lengths silver small cable chain
2 (2-inch) lengths 22-gauge silver wire
3¾ inches .018-inch-diameter nylon-coated flexible
   beading wire
Round-nose pliers
Chain-nose pliers
Crimp pliers (optional)
Wire nippers

Necklace

1) Cut faux-suede lace in half, forming two 7-inch lengths. Use chain-nose pliers to attach a c-crimp cord end to each end of faux-suede lace length. Open four jump rings and attach one to each cord end; close jump rings.

2) String a crimp end onto one end of 3¾-inch length of beading wire; use crimp pliers or chain-nose pliers to secure crimp end in place. Attach crimp end to one of the jump rings attached to faux-suede lace.

3) String the following onto beading wire: white cat's-eye bead, rose crystal, white cat's-eye bead, rose quartz bead, rose crystal and white cat's-eye bead. String on 1¾-inch shell pendant and repeat beading sequence in reverse.

4) String on remaining crimp end and crimp it to secure it to wire. Attach to a jump ring on remaining length of faux-suede lace.

5) Open a jump ring on end of necklace; attach half of clasp. Close jump ring. Repeat to attach other half of clasp to opposite end of necklace.

Earrings

1) Use round-nose pliers to form a wrapped loop at one end of a 2-inch length of 22-gauge wire, attaching loop to a 1-inch shell pendant before wrapping.

2) String a rose crystal and form another wrapped loop, attaching loop to an end link on a 1-inch length of chain before wrapping.

3) Open loop on ear wire and slide on remaining end link on chain; close loop.

4) Repeat steps 1–3 for second earring. ■

Pretty in Pink
Shell pendants from Lillypilly Designs; crystals from CRYSTALLIZED™ - Swarovski Elements; cat's-eye and rose quartz beads, beading wire, faux-suede lace and findings from Beadalon.

SIMPLY STYLIN'

Beaded head pins combine with silver chain for a fun, eclectic look.

Design | Jennifer Mayer Fish

Skill Level
Easy

Finished Sizes
Necklace: 18¼ inches (including clasp)
Earrings: 3¾ inches long

Materials
7 (10mm) crystal/silver/gold round beads
8 (6mm) green/gold round beads
11 white frosted E beads
14 silver bead caps
7 silver head pins
2 silver eye pins
11 silver jump rings
2 silver French ear wires
Silver spring-ring clasp with tag
Silver jewellery chain
Round-nose pliers
Flat-nose pliers
Wire nippers

Necklace

1) String the following onto a head pin: bead cap, crystal/silver/gold round bead, bead cap, two green/gold round beads and a frosted E bead. Use round-nose pliers to form a loop above top bead; trim excess wire.

2) String the following onto a head pin: green/gold round bead, bead cap, crystal/silver/gold round bead and a bead cap. Form a loop above top bead; trim excess wire. Repeat once.

3) Cut an 18-inch length of chain. Open a jump ring and slide on beaded head pin from step 1; attach jump ring to centre link of chain. Close jump ring with flat-nose pliers. Repeat with remaining beaded head pins, attaching them to either side of centre head pin, allowing equal space.

4) Open a jump ring and slide on clasp and one end link of chain; close jump ring. Repeat for opposite end of necklace, attaching tag.

Earrings

1) Cut two pieces of chain, one measuring 13 links and the other 7 links. Set aside.

2) String the following onto a head pin: frosted E bead, bead cap, green/gold round bead, bead cap and a crystal/silver/gold round bead. Form a loop above top bead; trim excess wire.

3) String the following onto a head pin: frosted E bead, green/gold round bead and frosted E bead. Form a loop above top bead; trim excess wire.

Simply Stylin'
Beads, ear wires and chain from
Blue Moon Beads; bead caps
from Cousin Corp. of America.

4) Open a jump ring and slide on the first beaded head pin and one end link of 13-link piece of chain; close jump ring. Repeat, attaching remaining beaded head pin to end link on 7-link piece of chain.

5) String the following onto an eye pin: frosted E bead, bead cap, crystal/silver/gold round bead, bead cap and a frosted E bead. Form a loop above top bead; trim excess wire.

6) Open a jump ring; slide on one loop of beaded eye pin and beaded chain lengths; close jump ring. Open opposite loop on beaded eye pin and slide onto ear wire. Close loop.

7) Repeat steps 1–6 for second earring. ■

CHERRY DELIGHT

Rose quartz is always pretty, even more so when nestled next to cherry agate.

Design | Katie Hacker

Skill Level
Easy

Finished Sizes
Necklace: One size fits all
Earrings: 1 inch long

Materials
18-inch strand 4.5–6.5mm graduated cherry agate barrel beads
3 (8mm) rose quartz round beads
3 (6mm) silver spacer beads
8mm silver jump ring
3 silver head pins
2 silver ear wires
1½ loops necklace memory wire
Round-nose pliers
Memory wire shears

Note: Memory wire is hard to cut and will damage regular wire nippers. Always use memory wire shears to cut wire coils.

Necklace

1) Use round-nose pliers to form a small loop at one end of memory wire, curving wire away from natural curve. *Note: Due to the strength of the wire, forming loops of memory wire may take some time.* String half of the barrel beads.

2) String a rose quartz bead and a silver spacer bead onto a head pin; form a wrapped loop above silver bead with round-nose pliers. Attach loop to jump ring; attach jump ring to centre of necklace.

3) String rest of beads; form a small loop on end.

Earrings

1) String a rose quartz bead and a silver spacer bead onto a head pin; form a wrapped loop above silver bead, attaching loop to ear wire before wrapping. Trim excess wire.

2) Repeat step 1 for second earring. ■

Cherry Delight

Cherry agate beads and rose quartz beads from Thunderbird Supply Co.; memory wire and findings from Beadalon.

AMETHYST DREAM

Glass beads in pretty shades of lavender add an eye-catching accent to any outfit.

Design | Katie Hacker

Skill Level
Beginner

Finished Sizes
Bracelet: 7 inches
Earrings: 1¼ inches long

Materials
28 (6–12mm) assorted purple glass beads
2 silver head pins
2 silver ear wires
9 inches (.8mm) transparent stretchy beading cord
Round-nose pliers
Wire nippers
Tape
Hypo cement glue

Bracelet

1) Place a piece of tape over one end of beading cord; string beads randomly. Remove tape and tie ends in square knots (Fig. 1).

Fig. 1
Square Knot

2) Place a drop of glue on knot; if bead holes are large enough, tuck knot inside nearest bead.

Earrings

1) String an 8mm and a 6mm bead onto a head pin; use round-nose pliers to form a wrapped loop above 6mm bead, attaching loop to ear wire before wrapping. Trim excess wire.

2) Repeat step 1 for second earring. ■

Amethyst Dream
Beading cord and findings from Beadalon.

LAPIS LAZULI

Ancient Egyptians used Lapis Lazuli as a symbol of truth. Early cultures valued these gemstones more highly than gold.

Design | Vicki Blizzard

Skill Level
Easy

Finished Sizes
Necklace: 22 inches (including clasp)
Bracelet: 8¼ inches (including clasp)

Materials
10 (8mm) lapis lazuli round beads
55 (4mm) sodalite round beads
12 x 18mm lapis lazuli chunk
91 (2.5mm) sterling silver cube beads
Bali daisy spacers: 130 (3mm), 24 (5mm)
4 (2mm) silver crimp beads
9mm twisted Bali silver jump ring
2-inch Bali beaded head pin
12mm Bali clasps: toggle with 2-link chain, lobster-claw
41 inches .015-inch-diameter 49-strand nylon-coated flexible beading wire
Round-nose pliers
Crimp pliers
Wire nippers

Necklace

1) For pendant, thread a large daisy spacer, the lapis chunk, a large daisy spacer and a cube bead onto head pin. Form a wire-wrapped loop above top bead and trim excess wire. Set aside.

2) Cut a 28-inch piece of beading wire. String a crimp bead and a cube bead ½ inch from end of beading wire; thread short wire end through lobster-claw clasp and back through beads. Use crimp pliers to flatten the crimp bead.

3) String a small daisy spacer, a sodalite bead, a small daisy spacer and a cube bead onto wire. Repeat 19 times.

4) String a large daisy spacer, a lapis bead, a large daisy spacer, a cube bead, a small daisy spacer, a sodalite bead, a small daisy spacer, a cube bead, a small daisy spacer, a sodalite bead, a small daisy spacer and a cube bead. Repeat once.

5) String a large daisy spacer, a lapis bead, a large daisy spacer, a cube bead, a small daisy spacer, a sodalite bead, a small daisy spacer and a large daisy spacer.

6) String pendant. Repeat steps 3–5 in reverse for second half of necklace.

7) String a crimp bead, a cube bead and the twisted jump ring. Thread end of wire back through several beads. Use crimp pliers to flatten crimp bead. Trim excess wire.

Bracelet

1) On remaining piece of beading wire, string a crimp bead and a cube bead ½ inch from end of beading wire;

thread short wire end through one half of toggle clasp and back through beads. Use crimp pliers to flatten crimp bead.

2) String 12 cube beads placing small daisy spacers between each. String remaining lapis and sodalite beads, starting and ending with a sodalite bead. Place small daisy spacers before and after each sodalite bead and large daisy spacers before and after each lapis bead, with cube beads in between.

3) String remaining 12 cube beads, placing a small daisy spacer in between each.

4) String a crimp bead, a cube bead and remaining half of clasp. Thread wire end back through several beads. Use crimp pliers to flatten crimp bead. Trim excess wire. ■

Lapis Lazuli

Gemstones from Fire Mountain Gems and Beads; cube beads, Bali spacers, toggle clasp, jump ring and head pin from Enchanting Beads; beading wire from Beadalon.

ASIAN STYLE

Add a touch of mystery and intrigue to your wardrobe with lightweight, Asian-influenced acrylic beads in warm shades of red!

Design | Vicki Blizzard

Skill Level
Intermediate

Finished Sizes
Necklace: 18 inches (including clasp)
Bracelet: 3 inches in diameter

Materials
2 large red flat faceted beads
Red chunky beads: 8 large, 15 medium, 12 small
8 (6 x 10mm) red diamond beads
41 (6mm) red round beads
133 (4 x 6mm) red bicone beads
40mm doughnut pendant
3 (2mm) silver crimp beads
2-inch silver head pins
Heavy silver toggle clasp
66 inches .018-inch-diameter 49-strand
    nylon-coated flexible beading wire
14 inches stretchy cord
Round-nose pliers
Chain-nose pliers
Crimp pliers
Wire nippers
Jeweller's glue

Necklace

1) For pendant dangle, cut a 6-inch length of beading wire. String 35 bicone beads. String a crimp bead. Thread opposite end of wire through crimp bead. Pull both ends of wire to shape beads into a circle; crimp the crimp bead.

2) Thread a bicone bead, a round bead and a flat faceted bead onto head pin; set aside. Attach beaded circle through centre of doughnut pendant with a lark's head knot (Fig. 1), positioning crimp bead so that it is behind doughnut and not visible from front. Form a loop at top of head pin, attaching head pin to bottom loop of circle of beads before closing.

Fig. 1
Lark's Head Knot

3) Cut remaining wire in half. String 35 bicone beads on both strands of wire, centring beads. Attach beads to pendant with a lark's head knot through doughnut. Thread all ends of wire through remaining flat faceted bead.

4) Separate wires into two groups of two wires and string one side of necklace as follows: two bicone beads, large chunky bead, medium chunky bead, three large chunky beads and four medium chunky beads.

Asian Style
Beads and pendant from The Beadery;
beading wire from Beadalon.

Separate wires again. *On one strand, string seven bicone beads; on other strand string three small chunky beads. Thread both wire strands through a diamond bead. Separate strands. On one strand, string seven bicone beads; on other stand, string five round beads. Thread both strands through a diamond bead. Repeat stringing sequence from *.

5) Thread both strands of wire through five round beads, a crimp bead, a bicone bead and toggle clasp. Thread ends back through the bicone bead, the crimp bead and several round beads. Pull ends and crimp the crimp bead. Trim wire ends. Repeat stringing sequence on other half of necklace.

Bracelet

1) String remaining medium chunky beads and round beads on stretch cord, alternating beads.

2) Tie ends of cord in a square knot (Fig. 2). Dot ends of cord with jeweller's glue; let dry. Trim ends. ■

Fig. 2
Square Knot

DECO DROP

Sport a glamorous vintage vibe with this bold Art Deco bracelet and matching earrings.

Design | Margot Potter

Skill Level
Easy

Finished Sizes
Earrings: 1½ inches long
Bracelet: 8 inches (including clasp)

Materials
6 (12mm) cream CRYSTALLIZED™ - Swarovski Elements crystal pearls
3 (9 x 6mm) black diamond CRYSTALLIZED™ - Swarovski Elements teardrop crystals
CRYSTALLIZED™ - Swarovski Elements bicone crystals:
   5 (6mm) light grey, 9 (4mm) black diamond,
   10 (4mm) black diamond AB
13 gunmetal eye pins
9 gunmetal head pins
4 (4mm) gunmetal jump rings
2 sterling silver French ear wires
Round-nose pliers
Chain-nose pliers
Flush cutters

Earrings

1) Open top loop on beaded teardrop eye pin and slide it on ear wire loop; close loop with chain-nose pliers.

2) Repeat step 1 for second earring.

Bracelet

1) Slide a pearl onto an eye pin; using round-nose pliers, form a loop above pearl. Trim excess wire. Repeat for each pearl. Set aside.

2) Slide a black diamond AB bicone crystal, light grey bicone crystal and a black diamond AB bicone crystal onto an eye pin; form a loop above top bead. Trim excess wire. Repeat four additional times.

3) Create a hook from an eye pin by using the thicker part of round-nose pliers to bend the wire over and the fine end of pliers to form a small loop at the end. Open a loop on a pearl eye pin; slide loop onto eye-pin loop on hook. Close loop with chain-nose pliers.

4) Open opposite loop on pearl eye pin and slide on a beaded eye pin; close loop. In same manner, continue attaching remaining pearl and beaded eye pins, alternating between pearl and beaded eye pins.

5) Slide a 4mm bicone crystal onto a head pin; form a loop above bead. Trim excess wire. Repeat for each 4mm bicone crystal. Slide a teardrop crystal onto an eye pin; form a loop above crystal. Trim excess wire. Repeat for each teardrop crystal.

6) Open a jump ring and slide on three bicone beaded head pins and one teardrop eye pin; close jump ring. Repeat for remaining beaded head and eye pins, setting aside two for use in the earrings.

7) Open another jump ring and slide on empty loop on remaining teardrop eye pin; attach jump ring to bottom loop on last pearl eye pin. Close jump ring. Slide hook into first jump ring to close. ∎

Deco Drop
CRYSTALLIZED™ - Swarovski Elements
from Jewelry Supply Inc.; gunmetal
findings from Rings & Things.

RIBBONS OF GOLD

You'll never be out of style wearing these dainty little classics with a sparkly twist.

Design | Caito Amorose

Skill Level
Intermediate

Finished Sizes
Necklace: 16¼ inches (including clasp)
Earrings: 1¾ inches long

Materials
5 (6mm) gold rhinestone rondelles
6 (4.5mm) gold rhinestone beads
Gold-filled jump rings: 2 (4mm), 1 (6mm)
2 gold-filled fishhook ear wires
7mm gold-filled spring-ring clasp
10¼ inches gold-filled chain
39 inches 26-gauge gold-filled wire
Dowel rod (optional)
Round-nose pliers
Chain-nose pliers
Wire nippers

Necklace

1) Cut three 6-inch lengths and six 1½-inch lengths of wire. Cut two 4⅛-inch and two 1-inch lengths of chain.

2) Thread one 6-inch wire through a gold rhinestone rondelle, centring wire.

3) Create left side of bow by making an approximately ⅝-inch loop with wire and threading remaining wire back through rondelle. Repeat on right side to make right side of bow. Trim excess wire tails as desired. If needed, bows can be smoothed and shaped carefully with a dowel rod.

4) Repeat steps 2 and 3 with remaining two 6-inch wire lengths to make a total of three bows. *Note: Bows do not need to be identical in width and length as variety will add interest to the design.*

5) Use round-nose pliers to form a wrapped loop at one end of a 1½-inch wire, attaching loop to one side of a wire bow before wrapping. Slide a rhinestone bead onto wire; form a wrapped loop next to bead, attaching loop to end link of a 4⅛-inch chain before wrapping. Trim excess wire.

6) Form a wrapped loop at one end of a 1½-inch wire, attaching loop to opposite side of wire bow from step 5 before wrapping. Slide a rhinestone bead onto wire; form a wrapped loop next to bead, attaching loop to end link of a 1-inch chain before wrapping. Trim excess wire.

7) Continue in the same manner as in steps 5 and 6 to connect remaining wire bows and chains. *Note: The 1-inch chains will be located in centre of necklace, while 4⅛-inch chains will be the sides of the necklace.*

8) Attach 6mm jump ring to one end of necklace; attach clasp to opposite necklace end.

Earrings

1) Open a 4mm jump ring and attach it to a gold rhinestone rondelle; close ring.

2) Cut a 6-inch length of wire. Thread wire through gold rhinestone rondelle from step 1, centring wire. Follow step 3 of Necklace to make a wire bow.

3) Open loop on ear wire and attach jump ring attached to rondelle; close loop.

4) Repeat steps 1–3 for a second earring. ■

SEAFOAM & SAND

This elegant set, inspired by fashionable jewellery designs, uses crystal pearls and silver-plated chain.

Design | Margot Potter

Skill Level
Easy

Finished Sizes
Necklace: 17½ inches (including clasp)
Earrings: 3¼ inches long

Materials
7 (12mm) light green CRYSTALLIZED™ - Swarovski
   Elements crystal pearls
7 (22-gauge) sterling silver eye pins
4 sterling silver jump rings
2 sterling silver French ear wires
Small silver toggle clasp
Small silver cable chain
Round-nose pliers
Chain-nose pliers
Flush-cut wire cutters

Necklace

1) Slide a pearl on an eye pin; use round-nose pliers to form a loop above pearl and trim excess wire. Repeat to make four additional pearl eye pins. Set eye pins aside.

2) Cut 18 (2¼-inch) lengths of cable chain. Separate lengths into six groups of three.

3) Open a jump ring and slide on one half of toggle clasp and one set of three chain lengths; use chain-nose pliers to close jump ring. Attach opposite ends of chain lengths to one loop on a pearl eye pin; close loop.

4) Attach another set of three lengths of chain to remaining loop on pearl eye pin. Continue attaching pearl eye pins and sets of chain lengths together in same manner. Use jump ring to attach remaining half of toggle clasp to ends of last set of chain lengths.

Earrings

1) Slide a pearl on an eye pin; form a loop above pearl and trim excess wire. Attach eye pin to ear wire. Secure loop closed with chain-nose pliers.

2) Cut three 1⅞-inch lengths of chain. Slide one end of each length of chain on a jump ring; attach jump ring to bottom loop on pearl eye pin.

3) Repeat steps 1 and 2 for second earring. ■

Seafoam & Sand
Crystal pearls from CRYSTALLIZED™
- Swarovski Elements; cable chain
and toggle clasp from Beadalon.

STRING QUARTET

Four variations on a bracelet theme are suitable for a night at the opera. Use whatever beads you happen to have on hand to create your own unique bracelet!

Design | Vicki Blizzard

Skill Level
Easy

Finished Size
7½ inches (including clasp)

Materials
Various metal castings featuring CRYSTALLIZED™ - Swarovski Elements crystals
Assorted small beads such as seed beads, bugle beads and small CRYSTALLIZED™ - Swarovski Elements crystals
4 (1mm) sterling silver crimp beads
2-inch sterling silver head pin (optional)
Silver metal toggle closure
19-strand nylon-coated stainless steel beading wire
Round-nose pliers (optional)
Chain-nose pliers (optional)
Crimp pliers
Wire nippers

Instructions
1) Measure wrist; add 6 inches to measurement. Cut two lengths of wire to this measurement. Hold ends of wires together and thread through two crimp beads, a crystal bead and straight end of toggle closure; thread wires back through crystal bead and crimp beads. Gently squeeze crimp beads and fold in half with crimp pliers; separate wires for remainder of stringing.

2) On each wire, string an equal number of beads and thread wires through metal casting. String an equal number of beads on each wire again. Repeat, alternating castings and beads, until beaded area of bracelet equals wrist measurement plus 1 inch; end with casting.

3) String an equal number of beads on each strand of wire. At this point, wires will be worked together as in step 1. Thread wires through two crimp beads, a crystal bead and through loop on remaining end of toggle closure. Thread wires back through crystal bead and crimp beads; gently squeeze crimp beads and fold in half with crimp pliers. Thread wire ends through several beads; trim excess wire close to beads.

4) For optional dangle: Thread desired beads on head pin. Use round-nose pliers to form a loop at top of beaded pin; attach loop to circle end of toggle clasp before closing. ■

String Quartet
Metal castings and crystals from
CRYSTALLIZED™ – Swarovski Elements.

CRYSTAL ELEGANCE

Give yourself flowers when you create this sparkly bracelet and earring set featuring silver rose spacer beads.

Design | Sandy Parpart

Skill Level
Beginner

Finished Sizes
Bracelet: 7½ inches (including clasp)
Earrings: 1¾ inches long

Materials
28 (4mm) clear crystal bicone beads
12 (4mm) orange crystal cube beads
13 (6mm) silver-plated rose-shaped spacer beads
2 (1½-inch) nickel-plated head pins
3 (4mm) nickel-plated jump rings
2 (1.3mm) silver crimp beads
11mm nickel-plated lobster-claw clasp
2 silver ear wires
10 inches .018-inch-diameter 7-strand
    nylon-coated flexible beading wire
Round-nose pliers
Flat-nose pliers
Crimp pliers
Wire nippers

Bracelet

1) String a crimp bead and lobster-claw clasp 2 inches from one end of wire; place short wire end back through crimp bead. Use crimp pliers to flatten and fold crimp bead.

2) String the following: crystal bicone bead, rose-shaped bead, crystal bicone bead and an orange cube bead. Repeat beading sequence nine additional times. String a crystal bicone bead, a rose-shaped bead and a crystal bicone bead.

3) String a crimp bead and jump ring; place wire end back through crimp bead and several other beads. Flatten and fold crimp bead. Trim excess wire.

Earrings

1) Slide the following onto a head pin: crystal bicone bead, rose-shaped bead, crystal bicone bead, orange cube bead and a crystal bicone bead. Use round-nose pliers to form a loop above top bead; trim excess wire.

2) Open a jump ring and slide on beaded head pin; attach jump ring to bottom loop on ear wire. Secure jump ring closed with flat-nose pliers.

3) Repeat steps 1 and 2 for second earring. ■

Crystal Elegance
Beading wire and crimp beads from Beadalon.

Aqua Dew Drops

A simple necklace chain provides the perfect foundation for easy and inexpensive jewellery.

Design | Lisa Galvin

Skill Level
Easy

Finished Sizes
Lariat: 21 inches
Earrings: 2½ inches long

Materials
8 (10 x 11mm) aqua Czech glass faceted fire-polished beads
5 (5mm) silver jump rings
4 silver eye pins
4 silver head pins
2 silver ear wires
Silver necklace chain kit (includes 24 inches 3mm cable and 18 inches 2mm round)
Round-nose pliers
Chain-nose pliers
Wire nippers

Note: If needed, use pliers to remove clasps from necklace chains.

Lariat

1) Cut a 1-inch length from cable chain; set aside to be used for earrings.

2) Slide an aqua fire-polished bead onto a head pin; use round-nose pliers to form a loop above bead. Trim excess wire. Open a jump ring and slide on beaded head pin; close jump ring. Repeat three additional times.

3) Open jump rings on beaded head pins and attach to first six end links on remaining length of cable chain, spacing them out for visual interest. Close jump rings.

4) Open remaining jump ring and slide onto cable-chain link 2 inches from opposite end. Slide last link of cable chain onto jump ring; close jump ring, forming a loop for lariat.

5) To wear, place chain around neck and bring chain through loop, adjusting it to desired hanging length.

Earrings

1) Cut eight pieces of round chain, each between ¼–½ inch long. Cut another 1-inch length of round chain. Cut 1-inch length of cable chain into two ½-inch lengths; set aside one ½-inch length to be used for second earring.

2) Open loop on an eye pin and slide on four of the ¼–½-inch round chain lengths. Close loop. Slide an aqua fire-polished bead onto the same eye pin; form a loop above bead. Trim excess wire. Repeat once.

Aqua Dew Drops
Beads and necklace chain kit
from Halcraft USA.

3) Open top loops of beaded eye pins and slide a ½-inch cable chain onto one loop and the 1-inch round chain onto the other; close loops.

4) Open loop on ear wire and slide on end links of beaded chains.

5) Repeat steps 1–4 for second earring. ■

RING BLING

This is a fast, fun and easy way to use up those favourite odds and ends. Create a new Ring Bling for every occasion! It's great for gift-giving too!

Design | Debbie Tuttle

Skill Level
Easy

Materials
2 (3–10mm) beads
6 inches 18- or 20-gauge dead-soft round wire
Ring mandrel
Diagonal wire cutters
Jewellery glue

Instructions
1) Locate ring size on ring mandrel; wrap wire snugly around mandrel three times. Remove wire from mandrel.

2) Gently pull wire ends away from centre wire.

3) Put a small amount of glue into holes of both beads.

4) Slide beads onto wire ends. Wipe away excess glue. Trim excess wire.

5) Let glue dry overnight. ◼

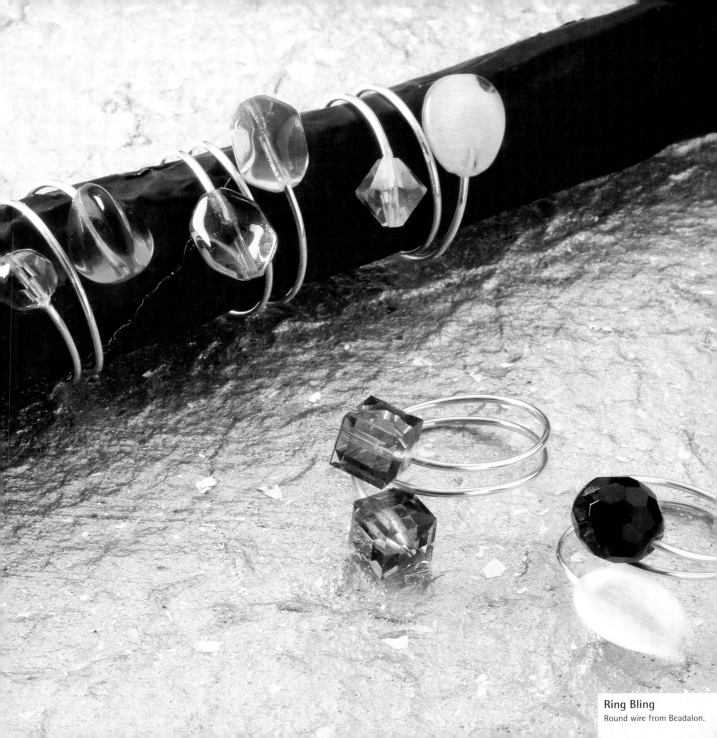

Ring Bling
Round wire from Beadalon.

BLUSHING BRIDE

Mother-of-pearl rings encircle delicate freshwater pearls perfect for the bride.

Design | Candie Cooper

Skill Level
Easy

Finished Sizes
Necklace: 18 inches
(including clasp)
Earrings: 1 inch long

Materials
13 (10mm) white coin pearls
26 (6mm) white potato pearls
14 (10mm) pink freshwater pearls
14 (3mm) pink button pearls
13 (25mm) mother-of-pearl pink doughnut beads
14 (10mm) silver bead caps
14 (1½-inch) silver ball-tipped head pins
2 (4.5mm) silver Scrimp findings
2 sterling silver ear wires
27.5mm sterling silver hook-and-eye clasp
25 inches .018-inch-diameter 49-strand
   nylon-coated flexible beading wire
Mini screwdriver (comes with Scrimp kit)
Round-nose pliers
Chain-nose pliers
Wire nippers
Jewellery glue (optional)

Necklace

1) Slide a pink freshwater pearl, bead cap and a pink button pearl onto a head pin; use round-nose pliers to form a loop above last pearl. Trim excess wire. Repeat 13 additional times for a total of 14 pearl dangles. Set two pearl dangles aside to be used for earrings. *Note: Bead caps should "cup" the freshwater pearls.*

2) String a Scrimp finding 1 inch from one end of beading wire; insert short wire tail through one half of clasp and back through Scrimp finding. Tighten Scrimp finding.

3) String a white potato pearl, one side of a pink doughnut bead, white coin pearl, other side of pink doughnut, white potato pearl and a pearl dangle from step 1.

4) Repeat step 3 twelve more times, but do not string last pearl dangle.

5) Insert wire through a Scrimp and other half of clasp; insert wire back through Scrimp. Adjust wire and tighten Scrimp. Trim excess wire. For additional security, add a dot of glue on top of each screw; let dry.

Earrings

1) Open loops on ear wires and slide on remaining pearl dangles; close loops. ■

Blushing Bride

Potato pearls and doughnut beads from Fire Mountain Gems and Beads; hook-and-eye clasp from Rio Grande; bead caps, Scrimp findings, beading wire and jewellery glue from Beadalon.

TIMELY TWISTS

It's always the right time for striking watches created with twisted wired beads.

Design | Beth Spicker

Skill Level
Easy

Finished Size
Approximately 7½ inches (including clasp)

Materials
4 (5mm) round beads
8 (6mm) Bali-style bead caps
8 (6mm) Bali-style beads
Watch face with large horizontal holes
2-strand box clasp with crystal inset
Half-hard round wire: 8 inches 18-gauge,
    12–16 inches 16-gauge
54 inches 18-gauge soft-twisted wire
Water-soluble marker
Jewellery file
Round-nose pliers
Flat-nose pliers
Flush cutters

Note: The holes in the beads and clasp need to fit over 16-gauge wire.

Instructions
1) Using flush cutters, cut two 4-inch pieces of 18-gauge half-hard round wire. File wire ends to remove rough edges and make ends flat. Mark centre of each wire length with marker.

2) Use tip of round-nose pliers to make a ⅛-inch loop at one end of wire, making it as round and smooth as possible. Grasp loop with flat-nose pliers and begin to form remaining wire around loop to form a coil. Continue coiling within ½ inch from centre mark on wire.

3) Slide a 5mm round bead onto wire; insert wire through hole in watch face. Slide on another 5mm round bead. In the same manner as above, form wire end into another coil approximately the same size as the first coil.

4) Repeat steps 2 and 3 for other side of watch face.

5) Lightly straighten 16-gauge half-hard round wire. Bend twisted wire in half and centre over 16-gauge half-hard round wire. Wrap twisted wire around 16-gauge wire once. Holding both wires with flat-nose pliers, proceed to wrap twisted wire around length of 16-gauge wire. Carefully pull 16-gauge wire out of wrapped-twisted wire. Cut four 1½–2-inch lengths of twisted wire; set aside.

6) Cut four 3–4-inch lengths of 16-gauge wire, making sure each length is the same size. File wire ends.

7) Form a loop on one end of one 16-gauge wire length. Slide a Bali-style bead and a bead cap onto one 16-gauge wire length; slide on one of the twisted-wire lengths from step 5, a bead cap and a Bali-style bead.

8) Form another loop at end of wire, making sure it is positioned in same direction as first loop so when placed on work surface, they lay parallel to surface. Gently bend beaded wire into a curve.

9) Repeat steps 7 and 8 for remaining three wire lengths.

10) Carefully open loops on one end of two wires; slide loops through holes on one spiral on one side of watch face. Close loops. Open opposite-end loops and slide on one half of clasp; close loops. Repeat with remaining two wire lengths, attaching them to opposite side of watch face. ■

CLEOPATRA'S COLLAR

The rectangular shape of the hematite and crystal pendant and the two-strand collar effect showcased in this necklace were inspired by jewellery from ancient Egypt.

Design | Carole Rodgers

Skill Level
Intermediate

Finished Sizes
Necklace: 17¾ inches (including clasp)
Earrings: 1¾ inches long

Materials
21 (3 x 13mm) double-drilled hematite bar beads
Crystal bicone beads: 12 (6mm) dark pink, 8 (6mm) pink,
    2 (3mm) dark pink, 12 (3mm) pink
Bali silver beads: 34 (2 x 4mm), 2 (4 x 6mm)
5 (2-inch) Bali silver head pins
2 (4mm) silver jump rings
8 (1.3mm) silver crimp beads
2 silver ear wires
Silver toggle clasp
40 inches .018-inch-diameter 19-strand
    nylon-coated flexible beading wire
Round-nose pliers
Chain-nose pliers
Crimp pliers
Wire nippers
Tape

Note: To secure beads while working, attach tape to wire ends not being strung.

Necklace

1) Slide the following onto a head pin: 3mm dark pink bicone, 2 x 4mm Bali bead, 6mm pink bicone, 4 x 6mm Bali bead, 6mm pink bicone, 2 x 4mm Bali bead and a 3mm dark pink bicone. Use round-nose pliers to form a wrapped loop above top bead; trim excess wire.

2) Slide the following onto a head pin: 3mm pink bicone, 2 x 4mm Bali bead, 6mm dark pink bicone, 2 x 4mm Bali bead and a 3mm pink bicone. Form a wrapped loop above top bead; trim excess wire. Repeat once.

3) Cut a 22-inch length of wire; slide the following onto the wire: 3mm pink bicone, beaded head pin from step 2, 3mm pink bicone, beaded head pin from step 1, 3mm pink bicone, beaded head pin from step 2 and a 3mm pink bicone. Centre beads and head pins on wire.

4) Pass one wire end through one hole on three hematite beads; pass other wire end through remaining holes on hematite beads, centring beads and head pins below hematite beads.

Cleopatra's Collar
Hematite beads from Wild Things
Beads; beading wire from Beadalon.

5) String a 4 x 6mm Bali bead onto one wire end; referring to Fig. 1, slide other wire end through same Bali bead, passing it through in opposite direction. This forms the centre of the necklace.

Fig. 1

6) Working on one side of necklace, string the following: 6mm pink bicone, one hole on three hematite beads, 2 x 4mm Bali bead, 6mm dark pink bicone, 2 x 4mm Bali bead, one hole on three hematite beads, 2 x 4mm Bali bead, 6mm pink bicone, 2 x 4mm Bali bead, one hole on three hematite beads, 2 x 4mm Bali bead, 6mm dark pink bicone and a 2 x 4mm Bali bead.

7) Repeat step 6 on opposite side of necklace.

8) String the following onto remaining 18-inch length of beading wire: 2 x 4mm Bali bead, 6mm dark pink bicone and a 2 x 4mm Bali bead. Pass wire through remaining holes on three hematite beads at one end of necklace.

9) String a 2 x 4mm Bali bead, 6mm pink bicone and a 2 x 4mm Bali bead; thread wire through remaining holes of next set of hematite beads. String a 2 x 4mm Bali bead, 6mm dark pink bicone and a 2 x 4mm Bali bead.

10) Thread wire through remaining holes of next two sets of hematite beads. Repeat beading sequences in steps 8 and 9, only in reverse.

11) String two crimp beads onto one end of top wire strand, approximately ½ inch from end; place wire end through one half of toggle clasp and back through crimp beads. Use crimp pliers to flatten and fold crimp beads. Repeat to attach other half of clasp to top wire strand.

12) Lay necklace on work surface and position bottom strand so beads lay correctly. String two crimp beads onto one end of bottom wire; place wire end through one half of clasp and back through the crimp beads. Flatten and fold crimp beads. Repeat to attach remaining end of wire to other half of clasp. Trim excess wires.

Earrings

1) Repeat step 2 of Necklace.

2) Open a jump ring and slide on a beaded head pin; attach jump ring to ear wire. Close jump ring. Repeat to attach remaining beaded head pin to other ear wire. ∎

POLKA DOTS ON PARADE

Tiny crimp beads add a little shimmer to this dressy duo. The interesting metallic beads are really earring backs!

Design | Lisa Galvin

Skill Level
Easy

Finished Sizes
Necklace: 25 inches (including clasp)
Earrings: 1¾ inches long

Materials
Pink glass polka-dot beads
Garnet button beads
Silver seed beads
50 (1.3mm) silver crimp beads
22 gold-tone bullet-style earring backs
2 gold 1-inch-long eye pins
2 silver ½-inch head pins
2 gold ear wires
Gold 2-strand filigree clasp
.015-inch-diameter 19-strand bronze nylon-coated
   flexible beading wire
Round-nose pliers
Crimp pliers
Wire nippers

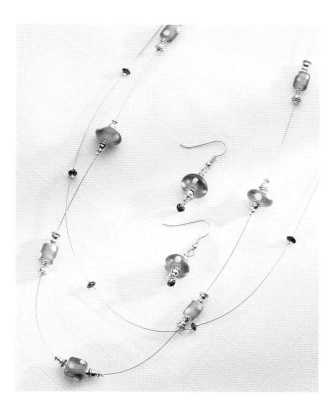

Necklace

1) Cut two 26-inch lengths of beading wire. String two crimp beads onto one wire approximately ½ inch from end; thread short wire end through a hole on one end of filigree clasp and back through crimp beads. Use crimp tool to flatten crimp beads.

2) String beads onto wire as follows: crimp bead, earring back, silver seed bead, polka-dot bead, silver seed bead,

earring back and a crimp bead. Repeat eight times, alternating direction of earring backs.

3) String two additional crimp beads approximately ½ inch from wire end. Thread wire end through one hole in remaining end of filigree clasp and back through crimp beads. Flatten crimp beads.

4) Referring to photo and beginning with centre set, adjust beads so sets are approximately 1½ to 2 inches apart. *Note: Each set will have a crimp bead on each end.* Flatten crimp beads next to earring backs to hold beads in place.

5) Connect second 26-inch length of wire to remaining hole in one end of filigree clasp in the same manner as in step 1. String a crimp bead, garnet button bead and another crimp bead onto wire; repeat sequence nine more times.

6) String two additional crimp beads onto wire approximately ½ inch from end. Attach wire to remaining end of clasp in same manner as in step 3.

7) Referring to photo, adjust bead sets so they align between polka-dot bead sets on other wire. Flatten crimp beads to secure placement of each set.

Earrings

1) Onto a gold eye pin, slide an earring back, polka-dot bead and another earring back. Use round-nose pliers to form a loop above earring back; attach to ear wire and trim wire end.

2) Onto a silver eye pin, slide a crimp bead, garnet button bead and another crimp bead. Flatten crimp beads to hold garnet in place. Form a loop above crimp bead; attach to bottom of beaded gold eye pin and trim wire end.

3) Repeat steps 1 and 2 for remaining ear wire. ■

Polka Dots on Parade

Beading wire, filigree clasp, crimp beads, eye and head pins from Beadalon; polka-dot beads from The Beadery; garnet button beads from Blue Moon Beads.

FROSTED ICE & SILVER

Available in many diameters, vinyl tubing can be found in your local hardware store. Use it to make your own beads and charms.

Design | Lisa Galvin

Skill Level
Intermediate

Finished Sizes
Necklace: 18½ inches (including clasp)
Earrings: 1¾ inches long

Materials
5-inch lengths of clear vinyl tubing in the following
   outer-diameter measurements: ¾ inch, 7⁄16 inch,
   5⁄16 inch, ¼ inch
200 silver seed beads
5 silver spool-shaped spacer beads
Silver round metal beads: 52 (4mm), 6 (6mm)
5 (2-inch) silver eye pins
6 (1-inch) silver head pins
Silver jump rings: 18 (6mm), 4 (9mm)
4 (1.3mm) silver crimp beads
2 silver ear wires
Silver hook-and-eye clasp
20 inches .018-inch-diameter 49-strand nylon-coated
   stainless steel beading wire
Cutting board
Craft knife
Round-nose pliers
Crimp pliers
Wire nippers

Necklace

1) String two crimp beads ½ inch from one end of beading wire; place short wire end through hook portion of clasp and back through both crimp beads. Use crimp pliers to flatten and fold both crimp beads.

2) String 100 seed beads onto wire. String 40 (4mm) silver round beads onto wire, followed by remaining 100 seed beads.

3) Slide on two crimp beads. Place wire end through eye portion of clasp and back through crimp beads and several other beads. Flatten and fold both crimp beads. Trim excess wire.

4) Using a cutting board and a craft knife, cut a ⅛–3⁄16-inch-thick slice of the ¾-inch-diameter vinyl tubing. Repeat to cut a slice of 7⁄16-inch-diameter vinyl tubing. Open a 9mm jump ring and slide on both pieces of vinyl tubing, nestling smaller piece inside larger piece; close jump ring.

5) Slide a 5mm silver bead onto a 1-inch head pin; use round-nose pliers to form a loop above bead. Trim excess wire. Open loop and attach it to 9mm jump ring attached to tubing, positioning head pin so it dangles inside small piece of tubing.

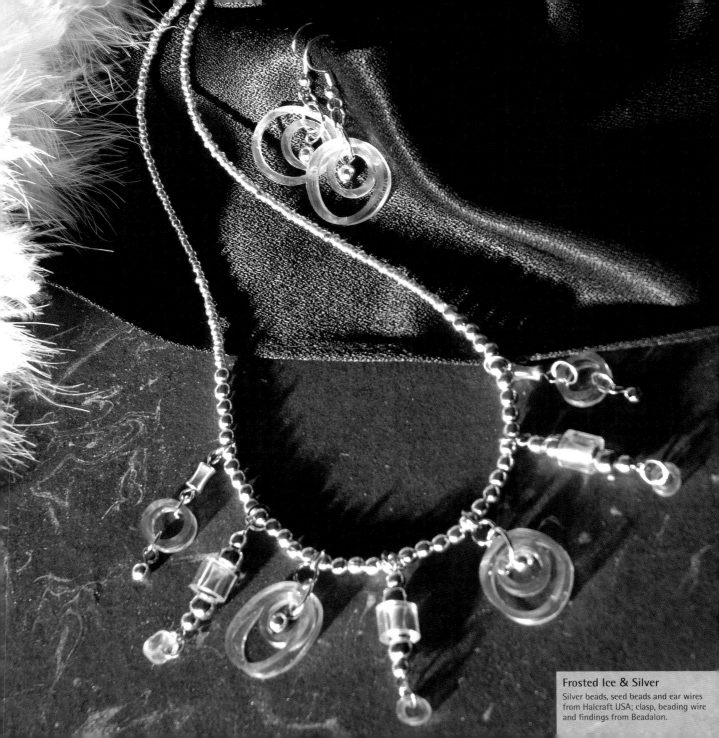

Frosted Ice & Silver

Silver beads, seed beads and ear wires from Halcraft USA; clasp, beading wire and findings from Beadalon.

6) Open a 6mm jump ring and slide it onto the 9mm jump ring attached to tubing; close jump ring. Set aside.

7) Repeat steps 4–6 to make a second dangle.

8) Slide a spool-shaped spacer onto a 2-inch eye pin; form a loop above bead. Trim excess wire. Cut a ⅛–³⁄₁₆-inch-thick piece of ⁷⁄₁₆-inch-diameter vinyl tubing; open a 6mm jump ring and slide on vinyl tubing. Attach jump ring to bottom loop of beaded eye pin; close jump ring. Slide a 4mm silver bead onto a 1-inch head pin; form a loop above bead. Trim excess wire. Open a 6mm jump ring and slide on beaded head pin; attach jump ring to vinyl tubing. Set aside.

9) Repeat step 8 to make a second dangle.

10) Slide a spool-shaped spacer inside one end of ⁵⁄₁₆-inch-diameter vinyl tubing; with spacer flush with end of tubing, cut tubing to match length of spacer exactly. Slide a 4mm silver bead, a 6mm silver bead, vinyl tubing spool-shaped bead, a 6mm silver bead and a 4mm silver bead onto a 2-inch eye pin. Form a loop above top bead; trim excess wire. Cut a ⅛-inch-thick slice of ¼-inch-diameter vinyl tubing; open a 6mm jump ring and slide on vinyl tubing. Attach jump ring to bottom loop of beaded eye pin; close jump ring.

11) Repeat step 10 to make two additional dangles.

12) Lay beaded necklace on work surface and arrange all of the dangles along centre section of necklace, evenly spaced. Use 6mm jump rings to attach dangles to necklace.

Earrings

1) Repeat steps 4–6 of Necklace to make a dangle; attach to loop on ear wire. Close loop.

2) Repeat step 1 for second earring. ■

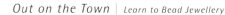

SWITCHABLES

Create a custom necklace or bracelet to fit your mood or outfit by switching these fun little charms.

Design | Molly Schaller

Skill Level
Easy

Finished Sizes
Necklace: 16¾ inches (including clasp)
Bracelet: 7½ inches (including clasp)

Materials
65 (5mm) white rice pearls
Focal beads: 2 millefiori squares, 2 turquoise nuggets,
   2 silver Bali-style round
Silver accent beads: 2 (18–20mm), 2 (12–13mm)
11 (2mm) silver round beads
Silver spacer beads in assorted styles: 16 (6mm),
   16 (4mm)
3 (2-inch) silver ball-ended head pins
4 silver crimp beads
6mm silver soldered jump ring
3 silver lobster-claw clasps
3 (2½-inch) lengths 24-gauge sterling silver wire
25 inches nylon-coated flexible beading wire
Round-nose pliers
Crimp pliers
Wire nippers

Necklace

1) Cut an 18-inch length of beading wire. String a crimp bead ½ inch from one end; place short wire end through

one clasp and back through crimp bead. Use crimp pliers to flatten and fold crimp bead.

2) String the following: 2mm silver round bead, 6mm silver spacer, an 18–20mm silver accent bead, 6mm silver spacer and a 2mm silver round bead.

3) String 51 rice pearls. Repeat step 2.

4) String a crimp bead; place wire end through soldered jump ring and back through crimp bead and several other beads. Flatten and fold crimp bead. Trim excess wire.

5) Slide the following onto a head pin: a 4mm silver spacer, a 6mm silver spacer, millefiori bead, 6mm silver spacer, 4mm silver spacer and a 2mm silver round bead. Form a wrapped loop above top bead. Trim excess wire.

Switchables
Rice pearls, millefiori squares and turquoise
nuggets from Fire Mountain Gems and Beads.

6) Repeat step 5 twice, substituting a turquoise nugget and a Bali-style bead in place of millefiori bead.

7) To wear necklace, attach clasp to soldered jump ring; slide desired beaded head pin onto clasp and fasten.

Bracelet

1) Repeat step 1 of Necklace with remaining 7-inch length of wire.

2) String the following: 2mm silver round bead, 4mm silver spacer, 12–13mm silver accent bead, 4mm silver spacer and a 2mm silver round bead.

3) String 14 rice pearls. Repeat step 2.

4) Repeat step 4 of Necklace, substituting remaining clasp in place of soldered jump ring.

5) Use round-nose pliers to form a wrapped loop at one end of a 2½-inch length of wire. String a 4mm silver spacer, a 6mm silver spacer, millefiori bead, 6mm silver spacer and a 4mm silver spacer. Form a wrapped loop above top spacer; trim excess wire.

6) Repeat step 5 twice, substituting turquoise nugget and Bali-style bead in place of millefiori bead.

7) To wear bracelet, attach clasps to looped ends of desired beaded wire. ■

WISDOM & MIRTH

*The cheery jingling coins and pendants
are matched up with some exotic
coloured, fun, reflective beads!*

Design | Jean Yates

Skill Level
Intermediate

Finished Sizes
Necklace: 17¾ inches (including clasp)
Earrings: 3 inches long

Materials
Pewter pendants: 2 owl coins, 5 "You are special,"
    4 Mirth coins, 2 turtles
Reflections lampwork beads: 3 (14.9 x 10mm) purple
    pink, 3 (15.5 x 8.5mm) pink, 2 (16.1 x 9.1mm) light
    topaz, 3 (15.3 x 9.3mm) gold topaz
Silver saucer beads: 20 (5mm), 2 (3mm)
Sterling silver snap-close jump rings: 10 (6mm),
    19 (8mm)
11 (3-inch) 22-gauge sterling silver head pins
2 (15mm) sterling silver French ear wires with bead
Sterling silver sunflower clasp
48 inches 5mm sterling silver rollo chain
Round-nose pliers
2 pairs of chain-nose pliers
Wire nippers

Necklace

1) Set aside two purple pink lampwork beads for earrings.

2) For long chain, slide a 5mm saucer bead, lampwork bead and a 5mm saucer bead on a head pin; form a wrapped loop. Trim excess wire. Repeat eight more times. These will be referred to as lampwork dangles.

3) Cut a 21-inch piece of chain. Determine centre link; use an 8mm jump ring to attach a pink lampwork dangle to centre link.

4) In the same manner, attach lampwork dangles to chain on left side of centre link as follows, skipping five links between each: light topaz, pink, gold topaz and light topaz. *Note: Attach all lampwork dangles so they hang from same side of chain.*

5) In the same manner, attach remaining lampwork dangles to chain on right side of centre link, skipping five links between each: gold topaz, pink, gold topaz and purple pink. Set aside.

6) For short chain, cut a 16¼-inch piece of chain.

Wisdom & Mirth
Chain, saucer beads, ear wires and Bernadette
Fuentes Reflections lampwork beads from Fusion
Beads; Snapeez jump rings from Via Murano;
pewter pendants and clasp from Green Girl Studios.

7) Open a 6mm jump ring and attach to one "You are special" pendant; close ring. Slide another 6mm jump ring onto first jump ring and attach to centre link of short chain, making sure the image is facing to the front. *Note: Attach all pendants so they hang from same side of chain.*

8) Attach one 8mm jump ring to an owl coin; skip one link from centre pendant and attach coin to chain. Repeat on other side of centre pendant.

9) Repeat step 7 on each side of centre pendant, skipping one link from each owl coin.

10) Attach one 6mm jump ring to a Mirth coin; attach to next link on chain next to last pendant with image facing to the front. Repeat on other side of chain.

11) Attach one 8mm jump ring to a turtle coin; skip two links from Mirth coin and attach turtle coin with image facing to the front. Repeat on other side of chain.

12) Use one 6mm jump ring to attach a Mirth coin to chain one link from turtle coin with image facing to the front. Repeat on other side of chain.

13) To assemble necklace, place chains on worktable making sure chains are positioned correctly (right sides of chains on right side, left sides on left side and short chain above long chain).

14) Open an 8mm jump ring. Slide end links on left side of chain onto jump ring; attach jump ring through loop on sunflower half of clasp. Close jump ring.

15) Repeat step 14 to attach leaf half of clasp to right ends of chains.

Earrings

1) Cut two 4-link pieces and two 7-link pieces of chain.

2) Slide a 5mm saucer bead, purple pink lampwork bead and a 3mm saucer bead on a head pin; form a wrapped loop, attaching loop to end link of one 4-link chain before wrapping. Trim excess wire.

3) Use an 8mm jump ring to attach "You are special" pendant to end link of 7-link chain.

4) Open another 8mm jump ring and slide on 7-link chain with attached pendant and 4-link chain with lampwork dangle. *Note: Place chains so drawn image of pendant is facing to the front and the longer chain is on the outside so it will hang farther away from face when worn. Attach jump ring to ear wire before closing.*

5) Repeat steps 2–4 for second earring. ■

CARVED CARNELIAN

The wearing of carnelian is recommended for those who have weak voices or are timid in speech. This set of rich olivine and serpentine greens is great for your autumn wardrobe.

Design | Terry Ricioli

Skill Level
Intermediate

Finished Sizes
Necklace: 21¼ inches (including clasp), plus a 6-inch dangle
Earrings: 1½ inches long

Materials
30 (4mm) olive green faceted glass tube beads
40 x 15mm carnelian carved oval bead
2 (15mm) Russian serpentine round beads
Tan with Asian script porcelain beads:
   5 (17mm) oval, 6 (11mm) disc
39 (4mm) antique copper rondelle spacers
7 (9mm) copper coiled rings
3 (2-inch) copper head pins
2 copper ear posts
2 ear backs of choice
Antique copper sunburst toggle clasp
25 inches 20-gauge copper wire
40 inches 1mm black leather cord
Round-nose pliers
Needle-nose pliers
Wire nippers

Necklace

1) Cut one 4-inch length and two 6-inch lengths of leather cord; these will be used for the centre dangle. Use remaining 24-inch cord for necklace.

2) Cut a 5-inch length of wire and form a wrapped loop ½ inch from one end; string two antique copper spacers, carved carnelian oval bead and two antique copper spacers. Form a wrapped loop above top spacer. Trim excess wire.

3) String beaded wire on centre of necklace cord. String an antique copper spacer and an olive green tube bead; repeat three additional times. String an antique copper spacer. Repeat on other side of cord. Tie a knot on each side, positioning beads so they sit next to beaded wire as shown.

4) Tie another overhand knot on one side of cord 2 inches from last knot. String an olive green tube bead, porcelain oval bead, copper ring, serpentine round bead, copper ring,

Carved Carnelian

Porcelain beads from The Beadery; carved carnelian bead and serpentine round beads from Fire Mountain Gems and Beads; olive green tube beads from Halcraft USA; spacers, copper coiled rings and clasp from Legendary Beads; ear posts and head pins from Blue Moon Beads; leather cord from Sulyn Industries Inc.; copper wire from Darice Inc.

porcelain oval bead and an olive green tube bead. Tie another overhand knot. Repeat on other side of cord.

5) Tie an overhand knot (Fig. 1) on one side 1½ inches from last knot. String two olive green tube beads, porcelain disc and two olive green tube beads. Tie an overhand knot. Repeat on other side of cord.

Fig. 1
Overhand Knot

6) String half of clasp, positioning it approximately 1½ inches from last knot; fold cord tail over and wrap both cords with a 4-inch wire. Wrap wire around cords five times; trim remaining wire and cord. Repeat on other side of necklace.

7) On one 6-inch cord, tie an overhand knot ¾ inch from end; string an antique copper spacer, porcelain oval bead and three copper rings. Thread cord through wrapped loop at bottom of centre dangle; string three antique copper spacers; knot cord ½ inch from end. Use a 4-inch length of copper wire to wrap the two cords together near wrapped wire loop with the porcelain bead side longer than the copper spacer side.

8) On second 6-inch cord, tie an overhand knot 1 inch from end; string two antique copper spacers, olive green tube bead and two antique copper spacers. Thread cord through wrapped loop at bottom of centre dangle; string a porcelain disc bead; knot cord ½ inch from end. Wire wrap cords together in the same manner as in step 7 with olive green side longer than porcelain disk side.

9) Tie an overhand knot ½ inch from end of remaining 4-inch cord. String an antique copper spacer and an olive green tube bead; repeat four additional times. Thread cord through wrapped loop at bottom of centre dangle; wire wrap cords together. Trim cord end close to wrap.

10) Slide an antique copper spacer, porcelain disc bead and three antique copper spacers on a head pin; form a wrapped loop above top spacer, attaching loop to wrapped loop at bottom of centre dangle. Trim excess wire.

Earrings

1) Slide the following on a head pin: antique copper spacer, porcelain disc, antique copper spacer, olive green tube bead, antique copper spacer, olive green tube bead and antique copper spacer. Form a wrapped loop above top spacer, attaching loop to ear-post loop before wrapping. Trim excess wire.

2) Repeat step 1 for second earring. ■

SUMMER LOVE

Fall in love all over again during the hot summer days and cool summer nights on the sand.

Design | Jean Yates

Skill Level
Easy

Finished Sizes
Anklet: 9¼ inches (including clasp)
Earrings: 2¼ inches long

Materials
6 (8/0) aqua silver-lined seed beads
3 (3mm) turquoise crystal bicone beads
10–12mm blue lampwork round bead
2 (7 x 2mm) sterling silver Turkish bead caps
5.5mm sterling silver alphabet block beads to spell
   desired name
2 (5.5mm) sterling silver heart block beads (optional)
Silver heart charm
2 (14 x 20mm) sterling silver palm tree charms
2 (3-inch) sterling silver head pins
4 (6mm) sterling silver snap-close jump rings
2 sterling silver ear wires with ball
7 x 11mm sterling silver lobster-claw clasp
8½ inches sterling silver cable chain
2 (5-inch) lengths 20-gauge sterling silver wire
Round-nose pliers
Chain-nose pliers
Wire nippers

Anklet

1) Open a 6mm jump ring and slide on another 6mm jump ring; attach ring to one end of chain. Close ring.

2) Slide alphabet block beads onto chain to spell desired name; add heart block beads if desired.
Note: If name is very long, use initials instead to keep amount of beads from being too heavy.

3) Slide a bead cap, lampwork bead and a bead cap on a head pin; form a wrapped head-pin loop above bead cap. Trim excess wire. Repeat with the following: aqua seed bead, turquoise bicone bead and an aqua seed bead.

4) Open a 6mm jump ring and slide on seed bead head pin; attach jump ring to end of chain. Open another 6mm jump ring and slide on clasp, heart charm and remaining beaded head pin; attach ring to previous jump ring.

Earrings

1) Slide palm tree charm onto a 5-inch wire ½ inch from one end; wrap short wire end above charm and wrap it around wire, forming a wrapped loop.

Summer Love
Palm tree charms, seed beads, bicone beads and block beads from Fusion Beads; bead caps, clasp, ear wires, chain, head pins and heart charm from The Bead Shop; lampwork bead from EJR Beads; snap-close jump rings from Via Murano.

2) Slide an aqua seed bead, turquoise bicone bead and an aqua seed bead onto wire. Form a wrapped loop above top bead; trim excess wire.

3) Open loop on ear wire and slide on top loop of beaded wire; close loop.

4) Repeat steps 1–3 for a second earring. ■

BACK TO NATURE

Many of these fun beads were recycled from vintage pieces found at garage and estate sales.

Design | Katherine McBee

Skill Level
Easy

Finished Sizes
Necklace: 18½ inches
Bracelet: Will accommodate small and large wrists

Materials
Carved bone elephant bead
Assorted shapes and sizes light- and dark-coloured beads
Assorted carved bone beads
Small natural-colour flat discs
Copper crimp beads
Copper toggle clasp with 2 holes
Silver head pin
2 (26-inch) lengths monofilament thread
1 (16-inch) length 0.5mm clear elastic thread
Round-nose pliers
Crimp pliers
Wire nippers
Masking tape
Jeweller's glue

Note: When stringing beads onto each strand, secure remaining strands to a smooth surface with tape.

Necklace

1) Slide a small bead, elephant bead and a small bead onto head pin; use round-nose pliers to form a loop above top bead.

2) Hold both strands of 26-inch lengths of thread and fold in half to determine centre. Thread elephant head pin onto centre of threads.

3) With both strands together, string the following on one side: small light-coloured bead, dark-coloured bead, carved bone bead, dark-coloured bead, carved rectangle, small carved bone bead, light-coloured bead, small carved bone bead, carved rectangle, small carved bone bead, small light-coloured bead and small carved bone bead.

4) Separate strands and string 12 flat discs onto each strand.

5) Hold strands together and string a small carved bone bead, small bead, small carved bone bead and four medium beads.

6) Separate strands and string 27 flat discs onto each strand.

Back to Nature
Copper clasp and crimp beads
from Blue Moon Beads.

7) Keep strands separate and string a copper crimp bead onto each one. Insert one thread end through one hole in one half of toggle clasp; run thread back through crimp bead and gently squeeze crimp bead. Repeat for other strand.

8) Repeat steps 3–7 for other half of necklace, attaching remaining half of toggle clasp at end.

Bracelet

1) Alternating between large and small beads, string desired carved bone beads onto 16-inch length of clear elastic thread.

2) Tie a double knot at end and secure with jeweller's glue. ■

SHINY SPOTS

We can't decide if these beads remind us of ladybugs or turtles. Whatever you think they look like, they'll add a bit of fun to any fashionable outfit!

Design | Vicki Blizzard

Skill Level
Easy

Finished Sizes
Necklace: 19 inches (including clasp)
Earrings: 1¾ inches long

Materials
7 (10 x 15mm) spotted black oval glass beads
Frosted E beads: 8 turquoise, 8 fuchsia
30 (1mm) sterling silver beads
6mm sterling silver jump ring
6mm sterling silver split ring
2 sterling silver clamshell knot covers
2 (2-inch) sterling silver head pins
2 sterling silver French ear wires
Sterling silver lobster-claw clasp
Black silk bead cord with attached beading needle
Round-nose pliers
Chain-mail pliers
Hypo cement glue

Fig. 1
Overhand Knot

Necklace

1) Do not cut silk cord. Referring to Fig. 1, tie two overhand knots at end of cord; apply a drop of glue and cover knot with a sterling silver clamshell. Tie a knot 3½ inches from clamshell. Thread a silver bead, turquoise E bead, silver bead, oval bead, silver bead, turquoise E bead and a silver bead; knot cord close to last bead. Measure 1½ inches from last knot and tie another overhand knot. Thread a beaded unit as before, substituting fuchsia beads for turquoise; knot cord close to last bead. Measure 1½ inches from last knot and tie an overhand knot.

2) Thread centre unit as follows: silver bead, fuchsia bead, silver bead, turquoise bead, silver bead, oval bead, silver bead, turquoise bead, silver bead, fuchsia bead and silver bead. Knot cord close to last bead.

3) Repeat measuring, knotting and beading sequence in step 1 in reverse; after last beaded unit, measure 3½ inches and tie a double overhand knot. Apply glue to knot; trim cord close to knot. Cover knot with silver clamshell.

4) Open jump ring and thread through hole in one silver clamshell and through hole in lobster clasp; close ring. Thread split ring through hole in other silver clamshell.

Earrings

1) On a sterling silver head pin, thread a silver bead, turquoise bead, silver bead, oval bead, silver bead, fuchsia bead and a silver bead. Form a loop at top.

2) Insert loop into hole of earring finding; close loop.

3) Repeat steps 1 and 2 for second earring. ■

Shiny Spots

E beads from Blue Moon Beads; findings,
ear wires, lobster clasp and bead cord
from Fire Mountain Gems and Beads.

ANCIENT ROMANCE

Fossilized coral makes a bold fashion statement with timeless appeal.

Design | Dianne de Vienne

Skill Level
Easy

Finished Sizes
Necklace: 18 inches (including clasp)
Earrings: 2½ inches long

Materials
20 (22 x 27mm) fossil coral teardrop beads
19 (6.5 x 7.5mm) bronze freshwater potato pearls
2 (6mm) gold-filled round beads
2 (1.3mm) gold crimp beads
2 gold-filled ear wires
2 gold-filled or gold vermeil soldered jump rings
Gold vermeil S-hook clasp
10 inches 24-gauge gold-filled wire
24 inches .018-inch-diameter nylon-coated flexible
   beading wire
Round-nose pliers
Chain-nose pliers
Wire nippers
Tape

Necklace

1) Attach a piece of tape to one end of beading wire.

2) String a crimp bead and a gold-filled round bead.

3) String a fossil coral bead and a pearl; repeat 16 additional times.

4) String a fossil coral bead, gold-filled round bead and a crimp bead.

5) Place wire end through a jump ring and back through crimp bead and gold-filled bead. Use crimp pliers to flatten and fold crimp bead. Trim excess wire. Remove tape and repeat on opposite end of wire. Attach clasp to one jump ring.

Earrings

1) Cut 24-gauge wire into four pieces, two 3-inch lengths and two 2-inch lengths.

2) Thread a 3-inch wire through a fossil coral bead, centring it; bring wire ends above bead so they meet in the centre. Use round-nose pliers to form a wrapped loop above bead with both wires; trim excess wire. Repeat for other 3-inch wire.

3) Form a wrapped loop at one end of a 2-inch wire, attaching loop to wrapped loop above a fossil coral bead before wrapping. String a pearl. Form a wrapped loop above pearl; trim excess wire. Repeat with other 2-inch wire.

4) Open loops on ear wires and slide on assembled pieces; close loop. ■

Ancient Romance

Fossil coral beads from Cherry Tree Beads;
pearls from Pizazz Works; beading wire
from Fire Mountain Gems and Beads.

MARDI GRAS

Celebrate the fun of New Orleans with themed charms, Mardi Gras colours and love.

Design | Dianne de Vienne

Skill Level
Easy

Finished Sizes
Chain Version: 16⅜ inches (including clasp)
Alternate Version: 18 inches (including clasp)

Materials
16 (12mm) Czech glass heart beads in amethyst, peridot and topaz
15 gold-plated pewter charms
32 (2mm) gold-filled round beads
32 freshwater pearls (optional)
2 gold oval-shaped beads (optional)
64 gold daisy spacers (optional)
2 gold crimp beads (optional)
16 (1½-inch) 24-gauge gold-filled head pins
17 (4mm) gold jump rings
Gold-filled lobster-claw clasp
Gold heart toggle clasp (optional)
24 inches .018-inch-diameter nylon-coated flexible beading wire (optional)
15¾ inches gold-filled link chain
Safety pin or paper clip
Round-nose pliers
Chain-nose pliers
Crimp pliers (optional)
Wire nippers

Chain Version

1) Determine centre link of chain and mark with safety pin or paper clip. Use a jump ring to attach a charm to centre link; remove marker.

2) In the same manner, use jump rings to attach remaining charms to chain, spacing them approximately 1 inch apart. There should be seven charms on each side of centre charm.

3) Slide a gold round bead, heart bead and a gold round bead onto a head pin; use round-nose pliers to form a wrapped head-pin loop above top bead, attaching loop to chain before wrapping. Trim excess wire. Referring to photo, repeat 15 additional times, attaching beaded head pins between charms.

4) Use a jump ring to attach lobster-claw clasp to one end of chain; attach remaining jump ring to opposite end of chain.

Alternate Version

1) Slide a gold round bead, heart bead and a gold round bead onto a head pin; use round-nose pliers to form a wrapped head-pin loop above top bead. Trim excess wire. Repeat 15 additional times.

Mardi Gras

New Orleans-themed charms from Gary's Arts, Crafts & Needlework Inc.; heart beads, gold-filled beads, head pins and clasp from South Pacific Wholesale Co.

2) String a crimp bead onto beading wire ½ inch from one end; place wire tail through one half of toggle clasp and back through the crimp bead. Use crimp pliers to flatten the crimp bead.

3) String a gold oval-shaped bead onto wire. String on a daisy spacer, pearl, daisy spacer, beaded head pin, daisy spacer, pearl, daisy spacer and a charm; repeat 14 additional times. String a daisy spacer, pearl, daisy spacer, beaded head pin, daisy spacer, pearl, daisy spacer and a gold bead.

4) String a crimp bead and remaining half of clasp; place wire end back through crimp bead and gold bead, pulling wire taut. Flatten and fold the crimp bead; trim excess wire. ∎

ROMANTIC DUO

An interesting twist of large black seed beads with traditional silver and turquoise form an elegant necklace and bracelet set.

Design | Vicki Blizzard

Skill Level
Easy

Finished Sizes
Necklace: 21½ inches (including clasp)
Bracelet: 7¾ inches (including clasp)

Materials
3 (9-gram) bottles opaque black 6/0 seed beads
37 (6mm) antique silver floral ring spacers
23 (8mm) antique turquoise melon pony beads
12 (10mm) antique turquoise melon corrugated
 ring spacers
3 (15mm x 12mm) antique turquoise filigree heart beads
8 (1mm) silver crimp beads
2 (2-inch) silver head pins
2 silver toggle clasps
19-strand nylon-coated stainless steel beading wire
Round-nose pliers
Chain-mail pliers
Crimp pliers
Wire nippers

Necklace

1) Cut three 30-inch lengths of beading wire. Thread all three wires together through a crimp bead, black seed bead, straight end of toggle clasp and back through black seed bead and crimp bead, leaving 1 inch of wire extending beyond crimp bead. With crimp pliers, gently squeeze crimp bead and fold it in half.

2) Separate wires; on each wire, string 15 black seed beads. Bring wires back together and thread through a silver spacer, melon bead, corrugated spacer, melon bead and a silver spacer (turquoise unit). Separate wires and string four black seed beads on each; thread all three wires through a silver spacer; separate wires and string four black seed beads on each (seed bead unit). Beginning with a silver spacer, repeat stringing sequence as described until four turquoise units and four seed bead units have been completed.

3) For centre unit, string wires through a silver spacer, melon bead, corrugated spacer, melon bead, melon bead, corrugated spacer, melon bead and silver spacer.

4) Beginning with a seed bead unit, repeat stringing sequence as described in step 2 until four turquoise units and four seed bead units have been strung; string 15 seed beads on each wire.

5) Holding wires together, string a crimp bead, a black bead and remaining end of toggle clasp. Thread wire ends back through black bead, crimp bead and seed beads. Gently squeeze crimp bead with crimp pliers and fold it in half. Thread wire ends back through several beads, trim excess wire.

Romantic Duo
Findings from Fire Mountain Gems and
Beads; bead stringing wire from Beadalon.

6) On silver head pin, slide a silver crimp bead, black seed bead, silver spacer, filigree heart, black seed bead, filigree heart, black seed bead and silver crimp bead. Form a loop at end of pin. Insert heart pendant between two turquoise units at centre of necklace; close loop.

Bracelet

1) Cut three 12-inch lengths of beading wire. Thread all three lengths together through a crimp bead, black seed bead, straight end of toggle clasp and back through seed bead and crimp bead, leaving 1 inch of wire extending beyond crimp bead. Gently squeeze crimp bead and fold in half with crimp pliers.

2) Separate wires; string four black seed beads on each wire and thread all three wires through a silver spacer (seed bead unit). String four additional seed bead units for a total of five seed bead units.

3) For centre unit, string a melon bead, turquoise corrugated spacer, melon bead, turquoise corrugated spacer and a melon bead.

4) String five seed bead units in reverse (starting with silver spacer).

5) Holding wires together, string a crimp bead, black bead and remaining end of toggle clasp; thread wire back through black bead, crimp bead and seed beads. Gently squeeze crimp bead and fold in half with crimp pliers. Thread wire ends back through several beads; trim excess wire.

6) For heart dangle, thread a head pin with a silver crimp bead, black seed bead, filigree heart, black seed bead and a silver crimp bead. Form a loop at end of pin; insert heart dangle on toggle closure and close loop. ■

MIDNIGHT SKY

Triple strands of snowflake obsidian separate and converge in a necklace that looks more complicated than it really is.

Design | Katherine McBee

Skill Level
Easy

Finished Sizes
Bracelet: Will fit small and large wrists
Necklace: 16½ inches

Materials
Small, medium and large grey/black beads
Grey/black chips
Bali spacer beads: 4 small, 4 medium
2 silver crimp beads
Silver-tone heart toggle clasp
3 (36-inch) lengths monofilament thread
3 (16-inch) lengths 0.5mm clear elastic thread
Crimp tool
Jeweller's cement
Masking tape

Note: *When stringing beads onto each strand, secure remaining strands to a smooth surface with tape.*

Bracelet

1) Holding all three 16-inch lengths of clear elastic thread together, string two large beads.

2) Separate strands and string three chips onto each strand.

3) Continue alternating between steps 1 and 2 until desired length is achieved. End with two large beads.

4) Tie a double knot; secure knot with jeweller's cement.

Midnight Sky

Chips, spacers, round beads and clasp from Blue Moon Beads; crimp beads and clear elastic from The Beadery.

Necklace

1) Hold the three 36-inch lengths of monofilament thread together; string a crimp bead onto one end approximately ½ inch from thread ends. Place short ends through one half of toggle clasp and back through crimp bead. Gently squeeze crimp bead with crimp tool.

2) Holding all three strands together, string two Bali spacers, small bead, medium Bali spacer, three large beads and a medium Bali spacer.

3) Separate strands and string three small beads onto each.

4) Hold strands together and string two large beads.

5) Repeat step 3.

6) Repeat step 4.

7) Separate strands and string three chips onto each strand.

8) Repeat step 4.

9) Continue alternating between steps 7 and 4 fourteen times.

10) Repeat step 3.

11) Repeat step 4.

12) Repeat step 3.

13) Join strands together and string a medium Bali spacer, three large beads, medium Bali spacer, small bead and two small Bali spacers.

14) Slide on a crimp bead and attach remaining end of toggle clasp in the same manner as in step 1. ■

VINTAGE BUDS

Glass leaf beads add a touch of sparkle to this delightful duo.

Design | Candie Cooper

Skill Level
Easy

Finished Sizes
Earrings: 1¾ inches long
Necklace: 16¾ inches (including clasp)

Materials
Gold round beads: 40 (3mm), 18 (4mm)
Glass leaf charms: 10 (13mm) green, 4 (25mm) green,
  4 (25mm) light green
10 (8mm) ivory faceted crystal round beads
8 red flower cloisonné beads
34 green E beads
Vintage flower button
2 gold eye pins
2 gold crimp beads
7mm gold jump ring
2 gold ear wires
Gold hook-and-eye clasp
22 inches flexible nylon-coated beading wire
Black fine-tip permanent marker
Dust mask
Safety glasses
Drill with #55 drill bit
Round-nose pliers
Flat-nose pliers
Crimp pliers
Wire nippers

Note: When drilling hole through vintage button, wear safety glasses and a dust mask.

Earrings

1) Slide a 3mm gold round bead, a cloisonné bead and a 3mm gold round bead onto an eye pin; use round-nose pliers to form a loop above top bead. Trim excess wire.

2) Open bottom loop of beaded eye pin and slide on a green 13mm leaf charm; close loop. Open top loop and attach it to ear wire; close loop.

3) Repeat steps 1 and 2 for second earring.

Necklace

1) Use black marker to mark a small dot near centre top of vintage button; use drill and #55 drill bit to drill through mark.

2) String a crimp bead ½ inch from one end of beading wire; place short wire end through one half of clasp and back through crimp bead. Use crimp pliers to flatten and fold the crimp bead.

Vintage Buds
Glass leaf charms and beads from
Fire Mountain Gems and Beads.

3) String the following onto wire: 3mm gold round bead, three 4mm gold round beads, a 3mm gold round bead, 13mm green leaf charm, a 3mm gold round bead and an E bead.

4) String an ivory crystal bead, an E bead, a 3mm gold round bead, a 13mm green leaf charm, a 3mm gold round bead and an E bead; repeat twice.

5) String a 4mm gold round bead, a cloisonné bead and a 4mm gold round bead.

6) String an E bead, a 3mm gold round bead, a 25mm light green charm, a 3mm gold round bead, an E bead, an ivory crystal bead, an E bead, a 3mm gold round bead, a 25mm green leaf charm, a 3mm gold round bead and an E bead.

7) Repeat step 5.

8) Repeat step 6.

9) Repeat step 5. String on an E bead, a 3mm gold round bead and an E bead.

10) Repeat beading sequences in steps 3–9, but in reverse to complete remaining half of necklace.

11) String a crimp bead and remaining half of clasp; place wire end back through crimp bead and several other beads. Flatten and fold the crimp bead. Trim excess wire.

12) Open jump ring and slide on vintage button; attach jump ring centred on necklace. Close jump ring ■

TRIBAL TEXTURES

Blended shades of polymer clay combine for a look that's undeniably tribal.

Design | Laurie D'Ambrosio

Skill Level
Easy

Finished Sizes
Necklace: 21 inches (including clasp)
Anklet: 9½ inches (including clasp)

Materials
Polymer clay: white, yellow, brown
2mm light brown leather necklace kit
4 topaz painted pony beads
Flat-nose pliers
Flush-cut pliers
Brown acrylic paint
Texture plate
Slicing blade
Barbecue skewer
Card stock
Disposable pan
Aluminum foil

Note: Materials listed are for brown set only.

Instructions
1) Condition clay; use one cherry-tomato-size ball of white and a pea-size amount each of brown and yellow. Thoroughly combine all colours.

2) Divide clay into thirds; two-thirds for necklace and one-third for anklet.

3) Roll one section of clay in palm of your hand to remove seams and air bubbles; slide it onto the skewer.

4) Flatten clay into a long bead shape by rolling it between your hands while it is still on the skewer.

5) Wrap texture plate around bead and squeeze to create a deep texture; roll plate on clay between your fingers to keep bead's shape; carefully trim ends of bead with slicing blade while bead is still on skewer.

6) Remove bead from skewer and gently curve it. Rub a small amount of paint with your finger onto bead to antique it.

7) Repeat process for anklet bead.

8) Lay card stock in baking pan; place beads on card stock. Cover pan with foil and seal sides; bake according to manufacturer's instructions.

9) To assemble jewellery, cut cord to desired lengths for necklace and anklet.

10) String a pony bead, clay bead and another pony bead; centre beads on cord.

11) Tie a knot on each side of beads to keep beads centred; trim cord if needed.

12) Add crimp ends and clasp to ends of cord; if crimped wire goes past cord, cut it with flush-cut pliers.

13) *Optional variation:* Marble black, white and metallic silver clay; leave it smooth. Use black pony beads and black necklace kit. Cut loops off of crimp ends and crimp them next to beads instead of tying knots. ■

Tribal Textures
Leather necklace kit from Darice Inc.

INSPIRE YOUR SPIRIT

These pretty charms make delicate music as they jingle together, reminding you to follow your dreams.

Design | Jennifer Mayer Fish

Skill Level
Easy

Finished Sizes
Bracelet: 8¼ inches (including clasp)
Earrings: Approximately 2⅜ inches long

Materials
13 gold inspirational word charms
Grey stone beads: 4 rectangles, 3 tubes, 2 chips, 8 round
Sliced stone beads
10 gold decorative spacer beads
Gold jump rings: 10 (7mm), 7 (3mm)
2 gold crimp beads
2 gold chandelier filigree earring findings
2 gold French ear wires
Small gold toggle clasp
.015-inch-diameter 49-strand nylon-coated flexible beading wire
Flat-nose pliers
Crimp pliers
Wire nippers

Bracelet

1) Open a 3mm jump ring and slide on a charm. Close jump ring. Repeat for six additional charms. Set aside.

2) Cut a 12-inch length of beading wire. String a crimp bead ½ inch from one wire end; insert short wire end through one half of clasp and back through crimp bead. Crimp the crimp bead.

3) Using an assortment of stone beads, spacer beads and charms, string beads as desired, positioning charms so they are evenly spaced.

4) Once bracelet is desired length, string a crimp bead and remaining half of clasp. Place wire end back through crimp bead and several other beads. Crimp the crimp bead. Trim excess wire.

Earrings

1) Open a 7mm jump ring; slide on two sliced stone beads, a charm and two sliced stone beads. Close jump ring. Repeat to make two additional beaded jump rings.

2) Open one of the beaded jump rings and attach it to bottom centre of chandelier finding. Close jump ring. In the same manner, attach remaining beaded jump rings to the right and left of first jump ring, allowing charms to overlap slightly.

3) Open another 7mm jump ring and slide on three sliced stone beads. Attach jump ring to the left side of

Inspire Your Spirit
Charms from Frost Creek Charms;
beads from Blue Moon Beads;
beading wire from Beadalon.

chandelier finding. Close jump ring. Repeat, attaching another beaded jump ring to right side of chandelier finding.

4) Open loop on ear wire; slide on beaded chandelier finding. Close loop securely.

5) Repeat steps 1–4 for second earring. ∎

COOL CORD ENSEMBLE

Trendy dots dance across beads in this fun-to-wear necklace and earring set.

Design | Debba Haupert

Skill Level
Intermediate

Finished Sizes
Necklace: 28 inches (including clasp)
Earrings: 2 inches long

Materials
Assorted sizes polka-dot glass beads
Antique silver spacer beads
2 small ear wires
Antique silver toggle clasp
Black round plastic cord

Necklace

1) Cut a 34-inch piece of cord; insert end through one end of toggle clasp. Using an overhand knot (Fig. 1), knot together by the clasp with about 2 inches extending from short end of cord. String a bead onto this short end and knot tightly.

2) Repeat step 1 on other end of cord with remaining half of toggle clasp.

3) Cut five 6-inch lengths of cord. Fold each piece in half and knot approximately ½ inch from fold; pull knot tightly.

4) Add one to three beads on each end of these cords and knot ends tightly; trim excess leaving ¼ to ⅜ inch cord hanging from knot.

5) String these five beaded loops on necklace over toggle clasp.

Earrings

1) Cut a 6-inch piece of cord; insert one end through loop on ear wire; knot together directly beneath ear wire.

2) Add a bead to each end; knot cords beneath beads and trim excess cord.

3) Repeat steps 1 and 2 for second earring. ■

Fig. 1
Overhand Knot

Cool Cord Ensemble
Polka-dot glass beads, spacer beads, ear wires and toggle clasp from Westrim Crafts; black round plastic lace cord from Toner Crafts.

MERMAID MAGIC

Wear the bracelets together on your wrist or clip them together to magically make one necklace.

Design | Candie Cooper

Skill Level
Intermediate

Finished Sizes
Coral & Pearl Bracelet: 8 inches (including clasp)
Charm Bracelet: 7¾ inches (including clasp)
Earrings: 1½ inches long

Materials
6mm pearls: 12 blue, 9 green
43 orange dyed coral chips
12 (3mm) gold/brown faceted glass oval beads
20 (5mm) gold daisy spacers
3 gold-plated ocean-themed charms

3 mini shells with holes
2 (25 x 22mm) gold mermaid charms
3 gold pinch bails
12 (5mm) gold jump rings
9 (2-inch) gold eye pins
6 (2-inch) gold ball-and-star–tipped head pins
2 (3.5mm) gold oval Scrimp findings
2 gold ear wires
2 gold mermaid clasps
10 (8mm) gold chain links
12 inches .018-inch-diameter 49-strand nylon-coated flexible beading wire
Mini screwdriver (comes with Scrimp kit)
Round-nose pliers
Chain-nose pliers
Wire nippers

Coral & Pearl Bracelet

1) String a Scrimp finding ½ inch from one end of beading wire; insert short wire tail through one half of one clasp and back through Scrimp finding. Use mini screwdriver to tighten screw.

2) String two coral chips.

3) String a daisy spacer, green pearl, daisy spacer and three coral chips. Repeat nine more times, alternating

Mermaid Magic
Mermaid charms from Fire Mountain Gems and Beads; mermaid clasps from ARTchix Studio; head pins, Scrimp findings, pinch bails and beading wire from Beadalon.

blue and green pearls; string only two coral chips on last sequence.

4) String a Scrimp finding; insert wire through remaining half of clasp and back through Scrimp; adjust wire and tighten screw. Trim excess wire.

Charm Bracelet

Note: Kitschy shell jewellery can be cut apart and the parts recycled into charms.

1) Slide a blue pearl onto an eye pin; use round-nose pliers to form a loop after pearl. Trim excess wire. Repeat eight more times, four times with blue pearls and four times with green pearls.

2) Open a chain link and slide on one half of clasp and one loop on a blue pearl link; close chain link. In the same manner, use chain links to connect all the pearl links to create a chain, alternating colours. Use last chain link to connect remaining half of clasp to last pearl link.

3) Slide one coral chip, gold/brown oval, coral chip, gold/brown oval, coral chip and a gold/brown oval onto a head pin; form a wrapped loop after last bead. Trim excess wire. Repeat three more times.

4) Attach a pinch bail to each mini shell.

5) Place bracelet on worktable and arrange shells, charms and beaded head pins in desired order. Use jump rings to attach shells, charms and head pins to bracelet links.

Earrings

1) Slide a blue pearl onto a head pin; form a loop above pearl. Trim excess wire. Repeat once.

2) Open loops on head pins and attach to top loops on mermaid charms, letting head pins dangle in centres of charms. Close loops.

3) Use flat-nose pliers to turn loop on each ear wire 90 degrees.

4) Open a jump ring; slide on top loop of a mermaid charm and ear-wire loop. Close jump ring. Repeat for other earring. ■

FUN & GAMES

Vintage game pieces just need a little modification to become fun, clever charms. It's a great excuse to use power tools!

Design | Candie Cooper

Skill Level
Intermediate

Finished Sizes
Charm Bracelet: 7¼ inches (including clasp)
Strung Bracelet: 8 inches long (including clasp)
Earrings: 1⅝ inches long

Materials
15 vintage Bingo chips*
15–20 beads in various sizes and shapes
Black round beads: 7 (4mm), 9 (6mm)
17 (2-inch) silver head pins
2 (1.3mm) silver crimp beads
2 silver ear wires
14mm silver toggle clasp
Silver bracelet link chain with clasp
10–12 inches .018-inch-diameter nylon-coated flexible
    beading wire
Black permanent marker
Clear semi-satin acrylic varnish
Safety glasses
Drill with #55 drill bit
Flat paintbrush
Round-nose pliers
Crimp pliers
Wire nippers
*Find vintage Bingo chips at flea markets and
    antique stores.

Note: Wear safety glasses when drilling through bingo chips.

Preparing the Bingo Chips
1) Place a dot at centre top of a bingo chip with permanent marker to mark hole placement. Carefully drill through bingo chip using drill and a #55 drill bit.

2) Brush a single coat of varnish onto bingo chip to enhance appearance and to protect it from wear. Let dry.

3) Repeat steps 1 and 2 for each bingo chip.

Charm Bracelet

1) Slide one or two beads onto a head pin; use round-nose pliers to form a loop above top bead. Trim excess wire. Repeat nine additional times.

2) Slide a bingo chip and a 4mm black round bead onto a head pin; use round-nose pliers to form a wrapped loop above top bead, attaching loop to centre link of bracelet chain before wrapping. Trim excess wire. *Note: If bracelet has links that are not soldered, form wrapped loop and then open link and slide on head pin. Close link.*

3) Repeat step 2 twice, attaching head pins to links near end of bracelet.

4) Slide a 4mm black round bead and a bingo chip onto a head pin; form a wrapped loop above bingo chip, attaching loop to one of the bracelet links. Repeat once, attaching it to bracelet so bracelet is balanced.

5) Open loops on beaded head pins from step 1 and attach to bracelet as desired; close loops.

Strung Bracelet

1) String a crimp bead onto beading wire ½ inch from end; place short wire end through one half of clasp and back through crimp bead. Use crimp pliers to flatten and fold crimp bead.

2) String a 6mm black round bead and a bingo chip; repeat seven additional times. String a 6mm black round bead.

3) String a crimp bead; place wire end through remaining half of clasp and back through crimp bead. Flatten and fold the crimp bead. Trim excess wire.

Earrings

1) Slide a bingo chip and a 4mm black round bead onto a head pin; form a loop above top bead. Trim excess wire. Repeat once.

2) Open loops on ear wires and slide on beaded head pins; close loops. ■

Fun & Games
Beads, findings, ear wires and clasp
from Fire Mountain Gems and
Beads; beading wire from Beadalon.

BUTTERFLY GARDEN

String assorted beads onto head pins, then attach them to a blank expandable bracelet for a colourful addition to any outfit.

Design | Candie Cooper

Skill Level
Easy

Finished Sizes
Bracelet: 2⅛ inches in diameter
Earrings: 1⅝ inches long

Materials
15mm silver Cha-Cha bracelet form
10 (12mm) butterfly beads
10 (10mm) flower beads
Approximately 300 assorted beads in desired colours, including leaves, birds and flowers
Beads for earrings: 2 (12mm) butterflies, 2 green front-drilled leaves, 4 (4mm) blue faceted round, 2 (6mm) orange faceted round
127 (2-inch) silver head pins
2 silver French ear wires
Round-nose pliers
Flat-nose pliers
Wire nippers

Bracelet

1) String desired combination of one to five beads onto a head pin; use round-nose pliers to form a loop above top bead. Trim excess wire. Repeat for approximately 125 head pins, leaving two head pins for earrings.

2) Open loops on head pins and attach them to loops on bracelet form; close loops securely with flat-nose pliers.

Earrings

1) String a leaf bead onto a head pin; use flat-nose pliers to carefully bend head pin forward at a 90-degree angle so wire is at centre top of leaf.

2) String the following onto the same head pin above the leaf: orange faceted round, blue faceted round, butterfly and a blue faceted round.

3) Form a loop above top bead; trim excess wire. Open loop and slide it onto an ear wire; close loop.

4) Repeat steps 1–3 for second earring. ∎

Butterfly Garden
Cha-Cha bracelet and beads from
Fire Mountain Gems and Beads.

BOUNTY OF BUTTONS

Use buttons from the sewing aisle as beads and charms to make your own unique jewellery.

Design | Patti Cosby

Skill Level
Easy

Finished Size
8–8½ inches (including clasp)

Materials
Round buttons: 6 (14mm) black shank, 8 (14mm) white, 5 (23mm) black/clear, 4 (11.5mm) green, 4 (17mm) yellow, 5 (17mm) orange, 8 (12mm) cream, 8 (11mm) red
Silver jump rings: 6 (6mm), 3 (7mm), 8 (9mm), 38 (10mm), 5 (12mm)
2 silver lobster-claw clasps
2 (7½-inch) lengths silver jewellery chain with links
Round-nose pliers

Black & White Buttons

1) Open a 7mm jump ring and slide it onto a lobster-claw clasp; attach jump ring to one end of chain. Close jump ring. Open another 7mm jump ring and attach it to opposite end of chain; close jump ring.

2) Open a 12mm jump ring and slide on a black/clear button; do not close jump ring yet. Attach a 12mm jump ring to each black/clear button.

3) Beginning with second link, attach jump rings with black/clear buttons to chain evenly spaced. Close jump rings.

4) In the same manner, use 6mm jump rings to attach one black button between each set of black/clear buttons. Also, attach black buttons to first and last links on chain.

5) In the same manner, use 9mm jump rings to attach white buttons between black and black/clear buttons.

Colourful Buttons

1) Open a 7mm jump ring and slide on a lobster-claw clasp; attach jump ring to last link on jewellery chain. Close jump ring.

2) Open a 10mm jump ring and slide it onto a yellow button; close jump ring. Repeat with each yellow button.

3) Open a 10mm jump ring and slide it onto a green button and through jump ring attached to a yellow button; close jump ring, forming a dangle. Repeat with each green button.

4) Open a 10mm jump ring and slide it through second hole on one of the green button dangles; do not close jump ring yet. Repeat for each green button dangle.

Bounty of Buttons
Jump rings, clasps and chain from Fire Mountain Gems and Beads.

5) Open a 10mm jump ring and slide it onto an orange button; close jump ring. Attach jump ring to another 10mm jump ring. Repeat for each orange button. Set aside.

6) In the same manner, attach a 10mm jump ring to each red and cream button.

7) Beginning with the second link, attach buttons to chain as follows: orange, cream, red, yellow/green dangle, red and cream. Repeat sequence three additional times. Attach remaining orange button. ■

TWILIGHT SKY

Iridescent and silver beads add a touch of shimmer and gleam to this pretty seed bead set.

Design | Katie Hacker

Skill Level
Easy

Finished Sizes
Necklace: 16 inches (including clasp)
Earrings: 1¾ inches long

Materials
8 (6mm) assorted silver/grey accent beads
155 (8/0) iridescent blue seed beads
2 (6mm) matte grey cube beads
2 (6mm) transparent grey round beads
2 (4mm) round silver beads
2 (1.5mm) silver crimp beads
2 silver eye pins
2 silver head pins
2 silver ear wires
Silver torpedo clasp
17 inches .018-inch-diameter 19-strand nylon-coated
 flexible beading wire
Round-nose pliers
Crimp pliers
Wire nippers

Necklace

1) String a crimp bead ½ inch from one end of beading wire; place short wire tail through one side of clasp and back through crimp bead. Use crimp pliers to squeeze crimp bead and fold it in half.

2) String 24 seed beads onto wire; string an accent bead and 15 more seed beads. Repeat pattern, alternating accent beads with 15 seed beads, seven times ending with an accent bead.

3) String 24 seed beads and a crimp bead. Place wire through other half of clasp and back through crimp bead; squeeze and fold crimp bead with crimp pliers. Trim excess wire.

Earrings

1) Place a cube bead onto an eye pin; use round-nose pliers to make a loop. Before closing loop, attach to ear wire; close loop and cut off excess wire.

2) Place a grey round bead and a silver bead onto a head pin; make a loop above silver bead. Attach to wire; close loop and cut off excess wire. Connect to bottom of eye pin.

3) Repeat steps 1 and 2 for second earring. ■

Twilight Sky
Seed beads and accent beads from
Blue Moon Beads; beading wire, crimp
beads and findings from Beadalon.

MACRAMÉ MAGIC

The classic look of macramé gets a modern twist with oval bone beads and black leather.

Design | Katherine McBee

Skill Level
Intermediate

Finished Sizes
Bracelet: Adjusts from 8½–10 inches
Key Chain: 5¾ inches long

Materials
5 small oval bone beads
Alphabet beads
Black leather cords: 2mm, 1mm
32mm silver key ring
Tape

Bracelet

1) Cut one 24-inch length and two 72-inch lengths of 2mm leather cord. Find centre of each length and tie them together in an overhand knot (Fig. 1), leaving a ½-inch loop or larger depending on size of beads. Loop will need to be large enough that beads will fit through it, but not so large that beads will slip out of it easily.

Fig. 1
Overhand Knot

2) Tape loop to work surface; tape two shortest strand ends, which should be centred between the four longer strands, to work surface. These will be the base cords, which are the strands the other strands are knotted around. They will not be moved while knotting.

3) Make a square knot by crossing the right set of cords over the two base cords and under the two left cords, leaving a loop to the right (Fig. 2). *Note: Figures do not show both cords in each set to allow readability.* Cross the left cords under the two base cords and up through the loop

Fig. 2

Macramé Magic
Beads from Nicole Crafts.

(Fig. 3). Pull both outside cords to tighten. Cross left set of cords (which are now on the right side) under the two base cords and over the right cords (now on the left side), leaving a loop to the right (Fig. 4). Cross the right set of cords over the base cords and through the loop (Fig. 5). Pull both outside cords to tighten the knot.

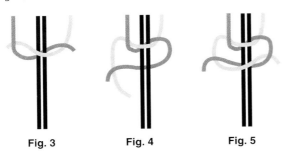

| **Fig. 3** | **Fig. 4** | **Fig. 5** |

4) Make five additional square knots.

5) String a bead on the right base cord; make a square knot.

6) String a bead on the left base cord; make a square knot.

7) Repeat step 5.

8) Make seven square knots.

9) Tie an overhand knot with all cords. Tie a knot on one of the base cords; string a bead. Tie another knot and string another bead; tie a

knot. Tie knots in the ends of remaining cords. Trim excess cord. Fasten bracelet by sliding beaded end of cord through large loop; adjust to size.

Key Chain

1) Cut one 9-inch length and one 48-inch length of 1mm leather cord. Holding cords together, fold leather cords in half; place folded end through key ring and thread loose cords ends back through formed loop and pull tight, securing cords to key ring.

2) Tape key ring to work surface; tape ends of two centre base cords down. In the same manner as in step 3 for bracelet, make six square knots.

3) String alphabet beads to spell desired name or word onto centre base cords. Make two square knots.

4) Tie an overhand knot with all cords. String a bead on each cord; tie an overhand knot and trim ends. ■

EXQUISITE EARRING TRIO

High-grade minerals, antique glass and crystal combine with quality findings for pieces that will garner compliment after compliment.

Design | Margot Potter

Crystal Bells

Skill Level
Easy

Finished Size
1⅝ inches long

Materials

2 (6mm) grey CRYSTALLIZED™ - Swarovski Elements diagonal-drilled cube crystals
4 antique German glass bell top-drilled beads
2 (22-gauge) sterling silver head pins
4 (4mm) sterling silver jump rings
2 sterling silver 3-loop round earring findings
2 sterling silver French ear wires
Round-nose pliers
Chain-nose pliers
Wire nippers

Instructions

1) Open a jump ring and string on a glass bell bead; attach jump ring to one of the bottom loops on round earring finding. Close jump ring. Repeat once.

2) String a crystal cube onto a head pin; use round-nose pliers to form a loop above bead. Trim excess wire. Open loop and attach to centre top loop on round earring finding.

3) Open loop on ear wire and attach to top loop on round earring finding.

4) Repeat steps 1–3 for second earring.

Purple Triangles

Skill Level
Intermediate

Finished Size
2¼ inches long

Materials

2 (12 x 12 x 14mm) amethyst flat triangle beads
4mm CRYSTALLIZED™ - Swarovski Elements bicone crystals: 6 lavender, 6 light green, 6 light blue
8 (2-inch) 22-gauge sterling silver head pins
2 (3 into 1) sterling silver spacer ends
2 sterling silver French ear wires
Round-nose pliers
Chain-nose pliers
Wire nippers

Instructions

1) Snip head off a head pin; use round-nose pliers to form a small loop at one end; string a purple triangle bead.

Exquisite Earring Trio
Azurite malachite beads, head pins and ear wires from Marvin
Schwab/The Bead Warehouse; spacer ends from Great Craft
Works; amethyst triangle beads and round earring findings
from Fire Mountain Gems and Beads; bell beads from Beads
and Rocks; crystals from CRYSTALLIZED™ - Swarovski Elements.

Form a wrapped loop above bead. Trim excess wire. Do not throw away wire remnants.

2) Form a loop on one end of a wire remnant. String a light blue bicone crystal. Form a loop above crystal and trim excess wire. Repeat with a light green bicone crystal. String a lavender bicone crystal onto a head pin; form a wrapped loop above crystal, attaching loop to bottom loop of light green bicone crystal before wrapping. Trim excess wire. Open top loop of light green bicone crystal and slide it onto bottom loop of light blue bicone crystal. Open top loop and slide it onto end loop on spacer end; close loop.

3) Repeat step 2 twice to make two additional beaded chains, attaching them to remaining loops on spacer end. Open top loop on spacer end and attach to bottom loop of purple triangle bead.

4) Open loop on ear wire and slide on assembled beaded dangle; close loop.

5) Repeat steps 1–4 for second earring.

Blue Squares

Skill Level
Intermediate

Finished Size
2 inches long

Materials
6 (8mm) azurite malachite puffy
   square beads
4 (2-inch) 24-gauge sterling silver head pins
2 sterling silver flat coil ear wires
Round-nose pliers
Chain-nose pliers
Wire nippers

Instructions
1) String an azurite malachite square bead onto a head pin; use round-nose pliers to form a wrapped loop above bead. Trim excess wire. Keep wire remnants.

2) Form a small loop at one end of wire remnant; string an azurite malachite square bead and form a loop above bead. Trim excess wire. Repeat once forming wrapped loops at top and bottom of bead.

3) Open loops on second beaded wire and attach remaining beaded wires; close loops. Open loop on ear wire and slide on beaded dangle; close loop.

4) Repeat steps 1–3 for second earring. ■

INDEX

INDEX

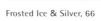

INDEX

INDEX

Alluring Fun

METRIC CONVERSION CHARTS

METRIC CONVERSIONS

yards	x	.9144	=	metres (m)
yards	x	91.44	=	centimetres (cm)
inches	x	2.54	=	centimetres (cm)
inches	x	25.40	=	millimetres (mm)
inches	x	.0254	=	metres (m)

centimetres	x	.3937	=	inches
metres	x	1.0936	=	yards

INCHES INTO MILLIMETRES & CENTIMETRES (Rounded off slightly)

inches	mm	cm	inches	cm	inches	cm	inches	cm
1/8	3	0.3	5	12.5	21	53.5	38	96.5
1/4	6	0.6	5 1/2	14	22	56	39	99
3/8	10	1	6	15	23	58.5	40	101.5
1/2	13	1.3	7	18	24	61	41	104
5/8	15	1.5	8	20.5	25	63.5	42	106.5
3/4	20	2	9	23	26	66	43	109
7/8	22	2.2	10	25.5	27	68.5	44	112
1	25	2.5	11	28	28	71	45	114.5
1 1/4	32	3.2	12	30.5	29	73.5	46	117
1 1/2	38	3.8	13	33	30	76	47	119.5
1 3/4	45	4.5	14	35.5	31	79	48	122
2	50	5	15	38	32	81.5	49	124.5
2 1/2	65	6.5	16	40.5	33	84	50	127
3	75	7.5	17	43	34	86.5		
3 1/2	90	9	18	46	35	89		
4	100	10	19	48.5	36	91.5		
4 1/2	115	11.5	20	51	37	94		

We have a sweet lineup of
cookbooks with plenty more in the oven

www.companyscoming.com